DALLAS
NORTH CAROLINA
A BRIEF HISTORY

Kitty Thornburg Heller

The History Press

Published by The History Press
Charleston, SC 29403
www.historypress.net

Front cover, top: Randall Jones Courthouse Painting, 2013. *Courtesy of Randall Jones.*
Back cover, inset: Photograph of the bandstand on the Courthouse Square, ready for Dallas's Fourth of July Celebration, 2011.

First published 2013

Manufactured in the United States

ISBN 978.1.62619.163.1

Library of Congress CIP data applied for.

Notice: The information in this book is true and complete to the best of our knowledge. It is offered without guarantee on the part of the author or The History Press. The author and The History Press disclaim all liability in connection with the use of this book.

The secret is not in seeking new landscapes but in having new eyes.
—Marcel Proust

To my family: my parents, grandparents, great-grandparents and my daughters and grandchildren.

CONTENTS

PREFACE

It is remarkable to stand between generations and to know one almost as well as the other. It gives you a perspective no one else has. You realize that you might be the only way your children and grandchildren will ever know their own family history.

For my parents, Kitty White Thornburg (1903–1998) and Clarence Otto Thornburg (1898–1989), whose ancestors were among the early pioneers of Gaston County and Dallas, I am very thankful they did get to meet and know their grandchildren, whom they loved. My mother was one of four sisters frequently called "the White girls." Iola and Leola—the twins—and Kitty and Allie White were the daughters of James H. White (named for his grandfather, a North Carolina state legislator for sixteen years) and Edna Mae Pasour White, youngest daughter of Simon Peter Pasour, a village blacksmith and furniture maker. My mother taught school for forty-two years in Gaston County, at Tryon, Costner, Dallas and Carr Elementary Schools (1921–65). Her home is still in our family and on the old White and Costner farms in Costner Community, the land of our forefathers. The house was built by my grandfather and great-grandfather White around 1905, two years after my mother was born. It is the farm where my mother grew up and where I grew up. My father was a farm boy who was born in Dallas Township at the turn of the century on a farm that, even then in 1898, had a history of three generations of Thornburgs behind it. Clarence was the oldest child of David Sylvanus Thornburg and Martha Ellen Pasour, daughter of David Rufus Pasour, Gaston County

Treasurer. D.S. Thornburg, son of L.A. Thornburg, was a dairy farmer who worked at the family sawmill, kept books for a cotton mill and was a 1909 postmaster and choir director. My dad was a teacher; a farmer; a World War I veteran; a builder of many homes, businesses and churches; and the general contractor for the North Carolina Orthopedic Hospital.

All four of my great-grandfathers—Thaddeus Sabiscy White, Simon Peter Pasour, David Rufus Pasour and Larkin Andrew Thornburg—fought in the War Between the States. Three lost one or more brothers during that war. Our family history and Gaston County history overlap.

ACKNOWLEDGEMENTS

I thank the people of Dallas for taking care of the old town treasures over the years—the homes and buildings we love—and recognizing their intrinsic value. You help make Dallas the special place it is today, and you are entrusted with preserving our Dallas heritage—our beautiful old homes, buildings and landmarks for which our town is well known—for us and for future generations.

An important contribution to this book was made by the Dallas Woman's Club, which has allowed me to reprint recipes from its past cookbooks. The recipes have added tremendously to making this book a more valuable resource, as have the people who contributed their recipes. All recent photographs were taken by me. All older photographs are from my own personal collections, except where noted.

This book would not have been possible without the patience, love, understanding and know-how of my three daughters: Kythe Heller, Sonya Heller Irey and Ingrid Fricks. Kythe was there when I needed her to make edits and to encourage; Sonya urged me on with a smile, a good word and time to write; and Ingrid had a keen listening ear and excellent suggestions. They understood that this work was important to me, and they did everything they could to help me accomplish it. As always, I am very thankful for my family's support and proud of my daughters and grandchildren: Baxter, Olivia, Portia, Romeo and Max.

I gratefully thank the following people: family stories (credit is given for each story) are from my parents, grandparents and relatives and from the

A 1957 reenactment of teachers arriving at the Dallas courthouse for teacher institutes during the early 1900s. Performers on the stairs are Elizabeth Carpenter (as Muriel Bulwinkle) and Barbara Carpenter (as Pearl Lewis); beside the buggy are Kenneth Witherspoon (as Wert Summery), Kitty Kay Thornburg (as Corrine Puett) and Patsy Cearley (as Sarah Hoffman); seated in the buggy are Anne Walker (as Ida Rankin) and Peggy Hoffman (as Maggie Hall). *Courtesy of Cherryville Museum of History.*

collections of Madge Houser, Lillian Senter, Dalton Stowe, Hilda Queen, Corinne Puett, Winnie Thornburg, Beth Friday, Mitchell Carr, Eloise Falls, Randy Thomason and Pat Sherrill. I consider myself privileged to have known all but one of these people, though even her I met through her writing. I especially thank Robert Carpenter for being a very knowledgeable and encouraging teacher and, along with Robert, Coleen Cloninger Peeler, Elizabeth Carpenter, Annette Carrigan, Ginger Cloninger, Peggy Cearley and John White for being willing readers of this manuscript. Banks Smither, my commissioning editor at The History Press, I truly thank for helping me along the way and believing this book had merit and would capture the spirit of Dallas, as well as Julia Turner, for her many hours of help. I want to thank Allie Hall White Hoffman, my mother's sister, wife of Carl Lee Hoffman, charter member of Gaston County Historical Society and eighth grade teacher in Dallas for thirty-eight years. Every year, her students interviewed family and friends to research Dallas history and make books. Some of those books are in the Gaston County Library, and some were printed in Historical Society Bulletins or made into town plays. Her daughter, Peggy Hoffman Cearley, has shared some keepsakes, stories and writings.

INTRODUCTION

Dallas is a beautiful little town of fewer than five thousand people located in Gaston County, North Carolina, in the southwestern Piedmont area of the state.[1] For sixty-four years, it was the county seat of Gaston County (1846–1911),[2] experiencing the excitement and hardship of that time. Today, it is loved and cherished by those who live there and know it. For people who live in other parts of the state, Dallas represents a study in the history of a town that has not been re-created but has remained almost unchanged since the turn of the twentieth century. It is easy to picture its history by just walking down its streets.

A significant part of the town's history can be seen and enjoyed today in its gala events and festivals, from the concerts and parades around the Square to the caroling, egg hunts, picnics, reunions and good old-time foods. Where possible, I have included recipes of dishes that I know have been served for over a century and that continue to be served in Dallas today.

Recent pictures in the following pages are of historical homes and places as they look today (2010–13). The Courthouse Square and eight buildings and homes in the vicinity are listed on the National Register of Historic Places (NRHP). The ones clustered around the Courthouse Square make up the Dallas Historic District. Dallas Township holds additional treasures.

This brief history of Dallas is divided into four parts. Part I describes the history of the land and town before and as the county was formed and grew. Part II provides a more intimate portrait of some of the people who lived in the town, their homes, celebrations and foods. Part III brings

The old courthouse, the symbol of the town of Dallas, is the center of the Dallas Historic District. *Photo by author.*

you up-to-date with some of the places you can find in Dallas and Dallas Township today. Part IV includes old stories and some people of note who once called Dallas home.

PART I

THIS SAME LAND

1
BEFORE DALLAS

To really understand a time and place, consider its history and the hardships its people endured in arriving there. The western Piedmont section of North Carolina was settled by the Katapaus (Catawba tribe) and, before them, the Piedmont people, who were made up of different tribal groups descended from some of the ancient Sioux who had moved into the area long ago.[3] Over time, they became the Catawbas, one of the most important eastern Siouan tribes. A few people in Dallas do trace their heritage back to the Sioux.[4] Just before the mid-1700s, one hundred years before Dallas was founded, Scottish Highlanders, Scots-Irish and Germans began settlements in the Piedmont region, a wild frontier then called the Carolina Backcountry with no western boundary. As more people came into the area, the Catawbas diminished in number due to disease (the smallpox epidemics of 1738 and 1759)[5] brought by the newcomers, wars, raids by the Cherokees and the settlers and finally being forced to move farther west or farther south. Many went to a small reservation near Rock Hill, South Carolina. In 1993, the Catawba Indian Nation became a federally recognized Native American tribe and was compensated with a significant settlement by the federal government and State of South Carolina for its land claims.[6] Traces of the Catawbas' strength and presence can still be found in the Dallas area.[7] The land holds their secrets: a carved rock here, an arrowhead there or a bit of pottery uncovered as fields are ploughed each spring. A sixteenth-century Catawba town discovered in 2010 in Morganton, North Carolina, fifty miles northwest of present-day Dallas, is now an archaeology

The Piedmont Monadnock Forest and granite outcropping are near the top of Pasour Mountain, Dallas Township. *Photo by author.*

site.[8] For more information, an excellent resource on the Catawba people is the exhibit at the Schiele Museum in Gastonia, North Carolina.

Pioneer German families with names of Best, Boshaar (Pasour), Cansler, Frietag (Friday), Fronabarger, Hoffman, Hovis, Hoyl, Huffstetler, Kastner (Costner), Kiser, Klemmer (Clemmer), Kloninger (Cloninger), Lineberger, Mauney, Plonk, Rein (Rhyne), Rudisill, Thornburg, Weaver, Weidner (Whitener), Wyant, Zimmerman (Carpenter) and others came to the New World, many looking to escape political and religious persecution. They journeyed by ship across the Atlantic Ocean, a dangerous decision in itself. Many landed in Philadelphia and traveled west to find new homes in what we call the Pennsylvania Dutch section. Some went to York and down the Great Wagon Road south from Pennsylvania through the Shenandoah Valley, sometimes staying in an area they traveled through for a few years before continuing farther. Frequently, they settled near one another along riverbanks, such as the Catawba, the South Fork and Big Long Creek. The Boshaars came through the gap of a mountain ridge, once called Laboon, within Piedmont Monadnock Forest. The mountain, with its granite outcroppings, was later to be known as Pasour Mountain, the western boundary of what today is Dallas Township.[9]

The German pioneers tended to settle in the area that became the northern part of Gaston County while the Scots-Irish populated the southern region. George Pasour Sr. (1725–1818), one of the early settlers, built his house on the eastern side of the mountain named for him. An old church or meetinghouse was said to have been at the gap of Pasour Mountain, and George Pasour was buried in the graveyard of that church. The church burned, but it was rebuilt later at a nearby site after a number of years and was used about early 1900 as a church by black members of the community. When my mother was little, her family sometimes would walk up to the mountain and attend church there, seated in the back pews.

The storms were rough on the Atlantic, and many ships were pushed back almost to their starting ports. Diseases spread quickly through the ships. There is a story of three young Lineberger brothers—Peter, Lewis and John—who sailed with their parents from England to America. During the long and rough voyage, both of their parents died at sea, and everything they had, all of the family belongings, was stolen or taken by ship authorities. The brothers were among those who walked the Great Wagon Road to the area that became North Carolina looking for a better life, freedom and opportunity.[10]

The Scots-Irish came from Northern Ireland in the 1740s to escape poor economic conditions and religious intolerance, as they were largely Scottish Presbyterians surrounded by Irish Catholics. (Another key immigration period happened in the 1840s, during the potato famine.) They made their way west, either coming down from Pennsylvania or coming up the Charleston Route, traveling along the Cape Fear River Valley toward the Blue Ridge Mountains. When they found a rocky area with rolling hills that reminded them of the old country they had left behind, they stayed, built their log cabins and cleared enough land for farming. Some of the Highlanders kept pushing deeper into the mountains. The English, many of whom were already living along the older colonial coastal settlements, came on the Carolina Trade Route hoping for more land or a new start.

African slaves, enduring terrible hardships, were brought into North Carolina by early sea captains and traders and helped to build the state's economy in the eighteenth and nineteenth centuries.[11] The eight English lord proprietors who had been made landlords over the Carolinas by the king of England encouraged slavery, and plantation owners and others who needed laborers and servants bought the slaves.[12] In the late 1600s, the lord proprietors offered land and other incentives to settlers who brought slaves into the area. By 1729, the king had bought out the interest of seven of the proprietors, and only one, Lord Granville, was left. He had control over the northern third of North Carolina, so there were more slaves in the richer, more populated sections of the state from early times. However, many North Carolinians never owned slaves.[13] Some large farms, plantations, mills, foundries and other places of business where labor was needed had many, as did some homes. Thirty years before the federal government would make the same ruling, during the Revolutionary War, the North Carolina Provincial Congress met in 1774 and ruled that "after Nov. 1, 1774, the importation of African slaves shall cease," though this ban was lifted again in 1790.[14] Levi Coffin (1798–1877), a Quaker born in Guilford County, North Carolina, and one of the founders of the underground railroad, is credited with helping an estimated three thousand slaves escape to freedom before the Civil War.[15]

During the Revolutionary War era, the Tryon resolves was a local declaration that vowed to resist British policies and was signed on August 14, 1775, in Tryon County, now Gaston, a year before the Continental Congress's Declaration of Independence was signed in Philadelphia. The signers of the Tryon resolves included Jacob Kastner (Costner) and Frederick Hambright, both of whom owned land in what was to become Dallas Township. William Tryon, the colonial governor for whom Tryon County was named, was greatly disliked, and so the large county of Tryon was divided in 1779 into Lincoln and Rutherford Counties, with the part that was eventually to become Dallas Township in Lincoln County.[16]

The Revolutionary War began and came south. Following the Battle of Ramseur's Mill (Lincolnton), the Battle of Kings Mountain, considered by many to be the turning point of the Revolutionary War,[17] was fought and won on October 7, 1780. Lieutenant Colonel Hambright was one of the commanders of the South Fork Boys and took charge after the death of Major William Chronicle, who was killed during the first minutes of the battle. British general Charles Cornwallis finally surrendered to General Washington at Yorktown, Virginia, on November 18, 1781. The Revolutionary War was won, and a new country, the United States of America, was born.

In the aftermath of the war, in 1788, the North Carolina General Assembly passed an "Act to Encourage the Building of Iron Works in the State." This law provided to anyone willing to develop an ironworks ten years of tax-free business and three thousand acres of land. Swiss-born John Fulenwider, who lived in Rowan County with his family during the Revolution and who had fought in the Battle of Ramseur's Mill, accepted the offer and founded the High Shoals Iron Works on the South Fork River, later adding a smaller ironworks on Maiden Creek. A copy of his land grant is in the state archives in Raleigh. His ironworks produced some of the highest-quality iron in

America.[18] The *Washington Post* stated that Fulenwider made and gave General George Washington a fine rifle in 1787.[19] The High Shoals Iron Works also made cannon balls for the War of 1812, which were floated down the Catawba River to Charleston on flatboats, along with other tools and cookware made of iron. When he died, Fulenwider had twenty thousand acres of land and many slaves. His youngest son, Jacob, built the tramway between the forge and mines on Long Creek and the Iron Works at High Shoals.

In 1799, gold was discovered in Cabarrus County when young Conrad Reed found a seventeen-pound gold rock in Little Meadow Creek near Charlotte. This was the beginning of the North Carolina gold rush, the first in the United States. At Kings Mountain in 1829, Mrs. Catherine Briggs—wife of Ben Briggs, who owned a smelter, iron mines and eleven thousand acres near Crowders Mountain and Kings Mountain and was soon to own a gold mine—found a gold nugget of very high quality in the bottom of her water bucket. This time prospectors came from Austria, Italy and Poland to try their luck.[20] Gold was also found at Pasour Mountain (Carter Hill Gold Mining Company) in the early 1830s.[21] The U.S. government decided to build a branch mint in Charlotte soon thereafter to make gold coins. William Groves Morris, a carpenter and millwright from Dallas who served as captain and lieutenant colonel of the Thirty-seventh North Carolina Regiment during the Civil War, hand made the wooden blinds for the windows of the mint, and they were of such fine quality that when the mint was closed, the blinds were saved. Gold from western North Carolina supplied the Charlotte Mint from 1837 to 1861. Lincoln County was growing fast with the discovery of gold. At the end of the Mexican War in 1848, the treaty with Mexico establishing the international boundary between the two countries was reported in the *Lincoln Courier* newspaper, and some people from Lincoln County went west to Texas to settle the new land. They had seen those wide-open spaces while they were fighting the war and couldn't resist. Many had been offered land grants for their military service. This made it even more attractive. One of the people who made that choice was James Pinckney Henderson, who later became the first governor of Texas. Some members of the Dallas Froneberger family, along with others, traveled west to Texas, too, and some even settled in what became Dallas, Texas, beginning the legend that Dallas, Texas, was named for Dallas, North Carolina. Included in the legend were letters that people of the town received telling of the naming of Dallas, Texas. Over the years, details and letters have been lost, and it has become just another story.

2
THE MAKING OF A COUNTY SEAT

The people in southern Lincoln County had a hard time getting to the county seat of Lincolnton when they had business there. Roads were bad, and the trip took a long time in a horse and buggy or by stagecoach. In 1846, James Hillhouse White, Larkin Stowe, Richard Rankin and F.D. Reinhardt were members of the North Carolina General Assembly from Lincoln County; the first three were living in the southern part of the county. After a difficult campaign, with White spearheading the effort, and finally by an act of the state legislature, Lincoln County was divided to make its lower (southern-most) region into a new county named Gaston, for William J. Gaston (1778–1844), a North Carolina lawyer, jurist, politician and U.S. congressman from New Bern, best known as the writer of the state song. Two of his most important judicial rulings were that a slave had a right to defend himself if his master attacked him without justification (1834) and that free blacks were North Carolina citizens and thereby protected by the state constitution (1838).[22] Most people in the state and country respected Judge Gaston.

A new county needs a county seat, and there was no town in the lower region of Lincoln County. So a new town was planned and created for that purpose. It was named Dallas, for the vice president of the United States under James K. Polk, George Mifflin Dallas (1792–1864). Dallas was a popular leader in the country at the time. As vice president, he presided over the Senate and signed the papers for the acquisition of Texas following the Mexican War. The land for the town of Dallas was purchased

Drawing of the Gaston County Courthouse by Sarah Hoffman Mauney in 1901. *Courtesy of the Gaston County Museum of Art and History.*

Long Creek Baptist Church was begun in 1772. The oldest grave has a date of 1728. *Photo by author.*

by commissioners from Gaston County from Jesse Holland, who graciously offered it to the town for the purpose of becoming the county seat. Isaac Holland II, chairman and one of the justices of the new county, along with Andrew Love, Jacob Plonk and W.F. Holland, surveyed the land and laid it off in lots. A courthouse and jail were built in 1847. The business of the town was set into motion as county officials were appointed on February 3, 1847, and took their places. The town was in full operation by 1847, but not until 1863, sixteen years later, was Dallas incorporated by the state of North Carolina.

When Zoe Brockman, noted North Carolina poet, journalist and author in the 1950s and lifelong resident of the county, told her story in the Gaston County Centennial Celebration play, *A Century of Growth*, she quoted Senator White's speech given at the historical meeting in 1846 at the home of Jesse Holland (the same home where Jesse's father had lived when he was the minister at Long Creek Baptist Church, not Jesse's new brick home, which was not built until 1847):

> *Gentlemen: The commissioners have arrived at their decision. This town of Dallas, so named for George M. Dallas of Philadelphia, Vice President of the United States under President Polk, shall be our county seat, in line with the stipulation that the county seat shall consist of 50 acres near the center of the county and not more than two miles from Long Creek Baptist Church. The county shall be called Gaston in honor of Judge William Gaston of New Bern, estimable gentleman and eminent jurist, who passed to his reward two years ago. The first county court will be held in this house on the third Monday of February, 1847. Gentlemen, the fate of Gaston County rests in our hands. May we give a good accounting to future generations!*[23]

The land grant actually says, "Seventy-five acres for the county seat of Gaston, called Dallas…for the sum of fifty dollars…signed, sealed and delivered in the presence of Ephraim Holland and James H. White. [Signed] Jesse Holland, February 20, 1847."[24]

During this same period of time while the county was being formed, the textile industry was beginning. The first three textile mills in Gaston County were Thomas Tate's mill at Mountain Island, the Lineberger's mill on the South Fork River near what is now Lowell and Jasper Stowe's mill at South Point, all built on the great waterways of Gaston County, the Catawba River and South Fork of the Catawba. In 1846, Henry Humphreys and a son-in-law, Thomas Tate, traveled from Greensboro to Gaston County and the Catawba River and bought land at Mountain Island for a mill that he had in operation by 1848. First called Lewis Lineberger and Company, Woodlawn Mill (or later known sometimes as Pinhook for the way the young women who worked at the mill fished in the South Fork) was started by Lewis Lineberger, his son-in-law Calab J. and Laban and John Lineberger, along with Moses H. Rhyne, Jonas Hoffman and John Clemmer. The Linebergers and the people who built the mill made everything themselves. Production began in 1852. Larkin Stowe, the senator, with his sons, Jasper, W.A. and Edward, bought land in 1846 at the area known as the Point and began production in 1853. These three mills were the forerunners of the textile industry in the county.[25]

There was unrest with the War Between the States approaching. South Carolina was the first state to leave the Union in January 1861, followed by Mississippi, Florida, Alabama, Georgia, Louisiana, Texas, Virginia, Arkansas and Tennessee. Shots were fired at Fort Sumter on April 12, 1861, and Abraham Lincoln called on North Carolina to send troops to help put down the rebellion to the south. North Carolina, the last state to do so, withdrew from the Union on May 20, 1861. Jefferson Davis (1808–1891), a West Point graduate who fought in the Mexican War, had been a United States senator from Mississippi and served as the secretary of war under President Franklin Pierce. He had spoken out against secession but was for a state's right to leave the Union. Mississippi decided to leave the Union, and so did Mr. Davis, who became the president of the Confederacy. Confederate soldiers from Gaston County, most white men between the ages of seventeen and fifty years old who were able to fight, fought in the War Between the States. Around 1,200 to 1,500 men left Gaston County to fight. Many lost their lives during the war. Those who returned home after the war faced, as most of the Southerners did, hard years of poverty and Reconstruction, during which time there was violence. Wesley Mauney and his wife, Naomi Wellman Mauney, built numerous churches and schools in Gaston County. When they started to build the first school for blacks near Long Creek Baptist Church in Dallas, the Ku Klux Klan said it would burn the school if it were built. The school was built, and the Klan burned it to the ground.[26]

Reconstruction was followed by the years of the railroad, years that would open up the country to trade and travel. According to historian Joseph Separk, in 1872, the citizens of Dallas very much wanted the Southern Railroad to come through the town and were excited by the prospect as the tracks drew nearer. They had recognized early the value of the railroad.

(At one time, before the Civil War, the town had come close to owning its own railroad, described in Part II.) But the commissioners did not allow it to happen, so the railroad went through the little community of Gastonia instead. Separk details how the event unfolded:

> *A story current in the '70s* [the 1870s] *and still believed by many is that a few citizens of Dallas prevented the Atlanta and Charlotte Air Line (later, the Southern Railway) from going through their town. The facts are as follows: Road authorities made proposition to the commissioners of that day if they would contribute a few thousand dollars toward the construction of the necessary bridges the road would come through that way. Interested citizens urged the commissioners to authorize a bond issue for the necessary funds. Commissioners refused. These citizens, led by Dr. Ephraim Holland, one of the sons of Jesse Holland, volunteered to contribute a part of their personal funds. Commissioners again refused and the railroad officials declined to come that way. It would have been cheaper for the road to have gone through Dallas than to have gone through the Whetstone Mountain route. That is the true story as related by one of close kin to the late Dr. Holland.*[27] [The Whetstone Mountain route was the route through Bessemer City.]

The records that Dallas, as the county seat, had on the commissioners' meetings, with their reasons for this decision, were burned in the Dallas courthouse fire of December 1874.

By 1874, A.P. Rhyne, Daniel E. Rhyne and Ambrose Costner started the county's fourth cotton mill in Mount Holly. Other mills in the county were starting as well. Schools were beginning. Dallas Academy became known as Dallas High School with M.L. Little as principal. The academy later became Gaston College and then Gaston Female College, with students from six states coming to Dallas for their education. Many of the early businesses, law offices and doctors' offices, stores and hotels were established around the Square. Peter Lineberger's blacksmith shop facing Holland Street was located behind J.R. Lewis's home, and John Lineberger had a home on the corner of Trade and Rhyne Streets with a blacksmith shop in back.[28] The town was growing.

3

TWENTIETH-CENTURY DALLAS

A significant incident in the history of Dallas was the campaign by citizens of Gastonia to have the county seat moved from Dallas to their town. The North Carolina General Assembly approved Act 455 in March 1909. It was "an act to allow the citizens of Gaston County to hold an election to express their will concerning the proposed removal of the county seat of Gaston County from Dallas to Gastonia and to remove the county seat as aforesaid, if the majority of the vote cast at said election shall favor such removal."[29] Gastonia officials had decided in 1889 that they needed to become the county seat or Gastonia's growth would be limited. They had meetings of citizens and town leaders and signed petitions that were not successful and did not come to a vote; however, five strong attempts were made with three resulting in a vote. Of the first two, one did not have the required number of qualified votes while the second one lost because most people expressed a desire to keep Dallas as the seat because it was created to be it. The third vote was handled differently. All that was needed was a simple majority. Two electors were assigned as judges in each precinct, one in favor and one against. The *Gastonia Gazette* ran notices reminding people that they had to register to vote twice a week for forty-five days before the vote. There were newspaper articles and public meetings. The last thing that was different was that a group of Gastonia's political leaders, merchants and mill owners pledged to give the county $43,000 if the vote came out in favor of moving the county seat to Gastonia. This money was to be used to pay for the new courthouse and jail that would be needed. Dallas leaders said they would give $21,000 to make updates and improvements to the existing courthouse and jail. On August 5, 1909, the bill passed in favor of Gastonia by a vote of 2,965 to 2,326, a majority of only 629 votes.[30] On January 1, 1911, the county seat was moved. The cost of the new county courthouse, according to the City of Gastonia, turned out to be $51,747, well over $43,000. For a few years, there were some hard feelings between the two towns as the names changed from "Holland, Hoffman, White, Lewis, Hoyle, Rhyne, and Friday in Dallas to Gray, Craig, Adams, and Love in Gastonia."[31] The vote was close considering that in 1910, Dallas had a population of 1,065 and Gastonia had a population of 5,759. The total population of the county was 37,063, but only the male portion of the county could vote.

In 1920, that changed with the passage of the Nineteenth Amendment to the United States Constitution. In 1919, the *Journal of Social Forces* stated that "the most powerful agency through which a woman has been able to express her individuality is through the Woman's Club movement."[32] In 1920, the Dallas Woman's Club had thirty-five members and held its meetings in the courthouse. Members donated to movements for the passage of the Nineteenth Amendment and campaigned for the rights of women. The first white woman from Gaston County to be elected to the North Carolina State Senate was Helen Rhyne Marvin in 1976. Senator Marvin served the state for sixteen years and worked tirelessly for women's rights, children, education and the poor. She received her master's degree in government in 1938 at Louisiana State University and was a professor of history at Gaston College in Dallas. She received the North Carolina Order of the Long Leaf Pine. The first black woman from Gaston County elected to the North Carolina General Assembly was Dallas-native Pearl Burris-Floyd, who served from 2009 to 2011 and was a member of the aging, health, appropriations and mental health committees. She is a graduate of the University of North Carolina–Chapel Hill School of Medicine and the senior advisor in the Office of the Secretary at the North Carolina Department of Health and Human Services.

As the textile industry grew, over 100 combed-yarn mills were established in Gaston County by 1920. That attracted attention. It was said that in textiles, where North Carolina goes, the South goes; where Gaston County goes, North Carolina goes; and where Loray Mill goes, Gaston County goes. The Loray Mill, at the time, was the largest textile mill in the South, and in 1923, it merged with a Rhode Island company, Manville-Jenckes. In 1929, the National Textile Workers Union was working for control. Two people were killed: Police Chief Aderholt while investigating a disturbance at the mill and Ella May Wiggins, a songwriter and millworker, while on her way to a labor rally.[33] National attention was focused on Gastonia. Pete Seeger recorded Wiggins's ballad "Mill Mother's Lament." The North Carolina historical highway marker erected beside the Loray Mill in 2013 reads that the strike "spurred opposition to labor unions statewide." However, the growth in the textile industry continued, eventually making Gaston County a world name in textiles. By Gaston County's centennial year, there were 140 textile mills. The textile exhibit at the Museum of Art and History in Dallas includes Thomas Edison's generator that was installed at the McAden Mill in 1884, the first mill to have electricity and the first generator installed in the South. It is thought that Edison installed it himself.

The Dallas Cotton Mill, the first textile mill in Dallas, was incorporated on March 9, 1891, by L.M. Hoffman, Jonas Hoffman, C.A. Campbell, J.R. Lewis, L.A. Suggs, John O. Rankin, M.H. Stroup and W.T. Henderson, and the mill later became Delcona in 1941 and Gibson Yarn and Weave Mill in 1948. On March 11, 1912, Robinson Mill Company was incorporated, and its name was changed to Robinson Yarn Mill. Morowebb Mills began in Dallas in 1904 with C.J. Webb, J.D. Moore, J.O. White, F.H. Robinson, E.L. Wilson and J.R. Lewis, and it became Gastonia Comb Yarn in 1945 and Macanal Textile Corp, New York Morowebb Mills in 1947. Monarch Mills was incorporated in Dallas on February 14, 1906, by R.S. Lewis, J.R. Lewis, S.A. Wilkins, J.W. Summey and M.A. Carpenter. The Dorothy Manufacturing Company was incorporated by S.M. Robinson, J.C. Rankin and C.E. Mason on March 11, 1912.[34] Federal child labor laws came with the Fair Labor Standards Act of 1938.[35] Up until that time, children were allowed to work in textile mills. These laws limited the age and number of hours young people were allowed to work, as well as who could work. The mills brought growth with people moving into the area seeking better jobs. The growth brought northern investors. In 1960, Dallas had 1,584 people employed in the textile and apparel industries and Gastonia had 8,670. Ruth Ann Lineberger was honored in the Gaston Centennial Book for having worked fifty years in one of the Dallas mills, Kirskey Sway for working fifty-four years and Robert Franklin Harris for working forty-eight years.[36] All three had worked in the Robinson Yarn Mill at one time. The Dallas mills were located near the Lenoir and Chester Railroad (later the C&NW) tracks, a convenient place from which to ship their goods.

Gaston County contributed volunteers for almost every war in the U.S. history. In the Battle of 1812, North Carolina furnished fourteen thousand soldiers, some from the Dallas area. In the Mexican War of 1846, there were eleven volunteers from Lincoln County (which included Gaston at that time), two of whom were killed and two of whom were wounded and later died. Gaston County furnished more soldiers to the Civil War than it had voters. (Seventeen-year-olds couldn't vote but they could fight.) In the Spanish-American War, about forty from Gaston County fought. In World War I, thirty-four men were killed, though it is not indicated how many fought. During World War II, thirteen young men from Dallas died fighting for freedom.[37] The war required the effort of everyone. Farmers grew more food. More people worked in mills and factories or in civilian war jobs. Schools sold war bonds and war stamps. Dallas hometown boy Charlie Thornburg served on the battleship *Missouri* during the war and witnessed the signing of the peace treaty for World War II. Dallas High School had a teacher, Mark Pasour, who was always the homeroom teacher for the senior class. He seemed to take it on himself to try to get in that last little bit of lifemanship training before students went out into the world on their own. Each year, he would give the graduating class a poem that he had written especially for them. In 1942, he decided to enlist himself, so he wrote a special poem: "But I want you to know, in the after years/In the time of toil, in the time of tears/Although the plains and the seas divide/I still am standing on your side."[38] He gave it to everybody that year, and years later, when he came home and came back to teaching, his words were still in his students' heads. That's how connected he was to his students. It takes the personal touch.

In the 1960s, the South had difficulty adjusting to *Brown v. the Board of Education* and the Civil Rights Act of 1964, but those places that were able to work for harmony, mutual helpfulness, equality and respect came out ahead. The leaders were those people who inspired everyone else to do the right thing, not by laws, though it has frequently taken them, but by personal example. Our schools changed, both physically and in their make-up. Now, we have W.C. Friday Middle School and North Gaston High School, and everyone goes, unless home schooling is chosen.

During the twentieth century in the United States, we went from the Wright brothers' first flight in 1903 to Neil Armstrong and Buzz Aldrin walking on the moon in 1969 in only sixty-six years, a little less than one normal lifetime. We went from no telephones, no television, no automobiles (for the average person) to cellphones, computers and Internet access for almost everyone. Who knows what the twenty-first century will bring.

PART II

SURROUNDED BY HISTORY

4

DALLAS COURTHOUSE (NRHP)

The Heart of Dallas

Standing in the center of the old Courthouse Square offers a 360-degree unparalleled view of Dallas history. The next chapters will continue the story of Dallas with a detailed portrait of the town's many historic buildings and personages, along with personal anecdotes and a tempting collection of favored town recipes.

The first courthouse was built in 1847 and was a temporary log house, replaced the next year by a red brick building with the steps inside. Abram Mauney had the contract for building the courthouse and jail. The fine handmade bricks were made on the lot behind the jail by slaves and freemen whose names have not been forgotten. The Hardy, Houser, Wellmon and Mauney families were some African American families who helped build many of the original buildings and homes of Dallas, especially those made of brick.[39] William Henry Houser went on to become a well-known brick mason and eventually owned his own company in Charlotte.[40] The homes, hotels and stores were beginning to be built as town lots were laid off and sold to raise money for the courthouse and jail. The lots were sold on April 6, 1847.[41] The first home built was Jesse Holland's brick house on the hill east of the Courthouse Square. The new house was a fine two-story brick home, the fifth brick house built in the county.[42] The four older brick homes were homes of General Joseph Dickerson (1778), Colonel James Johnson (1782), Thomas Rhyne (1799) and William Joseph Wilson (1812). Holland's new house was soon followed by the homes on the square. Those first homes built around the courthouse that still remain today make up the Dallas Historic District (National Register #73001344 entered on July 26, 1973).

The War Between the States

It was here in front of the red courthouse that the Gaston County Confederate soldiers, young men and old, ages eighteen to forty-eight and later seventeen to fifty, met to say goodbye to their families and friends before marching the seven miles to Brevard Station (Stanley) to board the train for Raleigh and receive their assignment for war—many never to return. It is thought that around 1,500, or about one-fifth of the white population of Gaston County, fought in this war. Some families had ten or twelve children, so frequently, several sons from one family fought. At the end of the war, on May 19, 1865, Colonel Wheeler's Union soldiers were camped on Courthouse Square and set up a headquarters in town. That winter, the Yankees bivouacked in snow and ice on the Square. Their main camp was set up in the yard of the Rush Dixon home place on the north side of town.[43] Dallas was still occupied by the North and would be for eleven more years. Today, there are two war memorials on the Square. One is a Civil War monument in front of the courthouse near Gaston Street that is inscribed with a list of the regiments that left from this spot. (Some of the Gaston County boys signed up in Lincoln County or Mecklenburg County, so this would not be a complete list of the regiments.) On the other side is the 1861 North Carolina flag. It is the Confederate North Carolina flag with the dates May 20, 1775, the date of the Mecklenburg Declaration of Independence, and May 20, 1861, the date North Carolina withdrew from the Union. North Carolina was very reluctant and voted against joining the Confederacy until the fighting (after the firing on Fort Sumter on April 12, 1861) had actually started and Abraham Lincoln asked North Carolina to send troops to support the war effort to invade the South and put down the rebellion. That was more than North Carolina could do. This monument was erected on May 4, 2003, by descendants of those who fought, making it a recent Confederate marker. The second war memorial on the Square is in memory of the nine young men of Dallas who sacrificed their lives in the Vietnam Conflict. They were Jerry Addis, Roy Neal Burris, Ronald Davis, Sherman Fields Jr., Anthony Long, Ronald Manuel, Rickey Mauney, Johnny Weeks and Donald Pasour.

The "Old Town Well" once provided water for the town. *Photo by author.*

In 1874, the red brick courthouse caught on fire, and the women in town ran out and gathered up court papers in their aprons as the building burned. Deeds and wills were saved. Most other records were lost. Court was held in the Rhyne Building, a store across Gaston Street, until the current courthouse was completed a year later in 1875 and built on what was left of the old walls and foundation. There is a well-known story of a Union soldier from Wisconsin, John Campo, who had enlisted in the Northern army in 1863. He was caught stealing a pair of shoes and jailed for his crime. Little Denie Lewis (Mary Modina Lewis Durham) was the one who saw him through a crack in the wall of her father's store, which was located near where the Dallas Paint Store is today. The crack was there specifically for keeping an eye on the Union soldiers. Mr. Campo was made to cut the stone for the 1875 courthouse steps, the granite fence and much of the stonework on the other homes and buildings in town and a few in the country. The stone came from near the White and Jenkins Mill. John Campo married Catherine L. Wyatt Jarrett around 1870, and they had three children.[44] His army company returned north in 1876, but Campo decided to stay to make Dallas his home, and he was a welcomed member of the community. He worked in the quarry and is buried in Long

The two meridian stones (one shown) on the Square were used by surveyors to calibrate their instruments. *Photo by author.*

Creek Baptist Church cemetery. The ornate banisters on the outside of the courthouse were made at the High Shoals Iron Works by Henry Fulenwider. In the early 1900s, the red brick walls of the courthouse were plastered with an exterior coating of concrete.[45]

The gazebo on the north side of Courthouse Square was a town well once. The two 1899 meridian stones, one on either side of the circular drive, are still on the Square (only one is pictured). These stones were used by surveyors to calibrate their instruments. Most counties had similar stones at the turn of the twentieth century, but now, more than one hundred years later, only two other North Carolina counties have meridian stones.

FESTIVITIES

Old Gaston College on South College Street held receptions and graduations on the lawn of Court Square during nice weather in the late 1800s and early 1900s. These were fancy occasions. Sometimes, as part of the celebrations, there were May Pole Dances, Square Dances and Cake Walks, and of course, there were picnics. Often, the young ladies made tempting lunches that they put in beautifully decorated boxes to be auctioned off to the young men. When a young man bought one of the boxed lunches, the young woman who made it ate lunch with him. Following the Civil War, "Old Soldiers Reunions" were held each year on the Court Square in nice weather or in College Chapel if the weather was stormy. Many of these reunions were planned and hosted by L.M. Hoffman, who had been too young to fight in the Civil War when it began, but in May 1864, he turned seventeen, enlisted and served in Company C, Seventy-first Regiment. At the same time, his father, Jonas, also had been in the Confederate navy. At the reunions, Miles Hoffman would have several pigs roasted for what would be called a pig pickin' and introduce a dignitary to speak. Families would come from all over the county, bands would play and people would pose to have their pictures taken. There would be games, stories and all sorts of festivities as old friends got back together, comparing and swapping their war stories.

In the spring, Easter egg hunts and egg fights were held here. For egg hunts, the eggs were hidden, and the children searched for them, as is still done today. For egg fights, two partners each held an egg in one hand with the large end up. Whoever went first tapped the other person's egg with his own egg. If it didn't crack, the other person took a turn. If one broke, they turned the eggs to the small ends and did the same thing with those ends. You continued with different partners until both ends were broken. The person who ended up with neither end broken won the egg fight and received a prize. (My family did this too, seventy years ago.)

TRIALS

If court was in session, there were debates and high drama. Sometimes, there were shouting matches across the Court Square as people disagreed over the outcome. People from all over the county would come to town in their wagons to watch.[46]

One frequently discussed trial was that of Caroline Shipp, the last woman executed by hanging in North Carolina and the last hanging in Gaston County, on January 28, 1892. She was sentenced to death after being found guilty of poisoning her young child to death, and she rode to the hanging tree sitting on top of her pine coffin. Many spectators—three thousand, it is said—from

100-Year-Old Recipe for Cookies

½ cup butter, softened
2 eggs
1 cup white sugar
1 cup brown sugar
2½ cups white flour
1 cup oatmeal
¼ teaspoon baking soda
½ teaspoon cream of tartar
1 teaspoon vanilla extract
1 cup nuts or raisins, if desired

Cream softened butter, eggs, white sugar and brown sugar in a mixing bowl. In a separate bowl, mix together the white flour, oatmeal, baking soda and cream of tartar. Combine both mixtures and add vanilla. You may add the nuts and/or raisins, if desired. Roll in balls and place on cookie sheets. Bake for 10 minutes at 375 degrees.

Recipe from Flossie E. Volke. Flossie Edison Volke had her own business catering fancy events in town. Good food was her trademark. (1954 Woman's Club cookbook.)

Hot Mulled Cider

2 quarts apple cider
2 cinnamon sticks
3 whole allspice berries
1 orange
8 whole cloves

Combine apple cider, cinnamon sticks and whole allspice berries. Stud the orange with the whole cloves and add to cider. Heat to boiling and then simmer.

Recipe from Mary Brown Robinson. Mary Brown Robinson worked at Belks in the cosmetic department and always looked beautiful. Her food does, too. (1954 Woman's Club cookbook.)

In 2011, "Carols on the Square," led by Mary Ann Friday Carpenter, brought together old friends and new ones. *Photo by author.*

all over the county came to watch. Some historians doubt her guilt, and many people at the time believed her boyfriend, Mack Farrar, was involved.

Another renowned trial, in 1899, involved Alfonzo Rhyne, who was accused of killing Mr. Falls of South Gastonia. Many people thought some might try to take the law into their own hands and have a lynching. The state guard was called in and stationed in Dallas until the trial was over.[47]

Back then, the most famous trial was the Kale-Carpenter murder trial. Mr. Kale was killed, and Mr. Carpenter was seriously wounded and not expected to live. The lawyers and the judge brought to Dallas for this trial were considered to be some of the best in the state. Each side had five or six lawyers. The murder took place in Hardin near the mill. According to the newspaper reports, the disagreement was over hiring employees and whether one was trying to encourage workers from another mill to come and work for him. Both were accusing the other. During the trial, many newspapers, including the *Charlotte Observer* and the *Star* paper in Columbia, South Carolina, ran daily front-page articles.[48]

Many things happened on the Square. It was the place to go to find out the news and to meet up with different people. At one time, there were church services held in the old courthouse when itinerant ministers were passing through, and high school farm life classes were given for young men preparing to make their way in the world, many to become tillers of the soil. The Dallas Woman's Club, one of Dallas's oldest organizations, began here and meetings were held upstairs. The women planned service events and social gatherings, and they quietly helped anyone who needed it. Now, there are many town get-togethers and events held on and around the Square, and more are always being planned.

An annual event called "Christmas Carols on the Square" is held with Christmas cookies, hot chocolate and hot mulled cider, provided for everyone by the Town of Dallas. At a recent caroling, a great-great-granddaughter of James Hillhouse White sang a solo while great-great-grandchildren of Colonel Morris, the Hoyles, Costners, Bests, Pasours, Cloningers, Fridays, Rhynes, Clemmers, Carpenters and others joined with friends and neighbors for the singing.

5
A WALK AROUND THE COURTHOUSE SQUARE

Take a walk or a ride around the old Square, perhaps in a Lewis Farm wagon such as this one. Court Square is surrounded by stories—it is the center of the town after all—but the homes tell you about the people who lived here; bound by history, these houses are welcoming to

Lewis Farm offers wagon rides around the Square during town fairs and festivals. *Photo by author.*

newcomers and old friends. The architecture and the history are intertwined, and if you know one, it helps to know the other.

TO THE SOUTH OF THE SQUARE

Hoffman House Hotel (NRHD)
131 WEST MAIN STREET (LOT 5)

The Hoffman House is believed to be North Carolina's largest and best-preserved mid-nineteenth-century hotel. It has been called "a perfect example of nineteenth-century inns."[49] This handsome three-story brick structure, which in 1980 became the Gaston County Museum of Art and History, was built in 1852 by Daniel Hoffman. Harold Lineberger and Daniel Stowe, both leaders in the textile industry, and many Dallas citizens made generous contributions and gifts to turn this building into a museum. Many antique furnishings used here were originally old family heirlooms brought with the Hoffman family from

The Hoffman House Hotel, built in 1852, is one of the largest, best-preserved mid-nineteenth-century hotels in North Carolina. *Photo by author.*

Recipes for Sunday Dinner

From the Hoffman Hotel, the aroma of good food filled the air as guests were served rice and gravy with country ham, biscuits and rolls and candied sweet potatoes.

Candied Sweet Potatoes

2 or 3 spoons of butter
2 or 3 sweet potatoes, thinly sliced
½ cup sugar
½ cup water

Heat butter in frying pan; add potatoes evenly and let simmer. Cover with sugar and cook until melted. Pour water over to make the syrup. Simmer until potatoes are soft.

Refrigerator Rolls

2 cakes yeast
¼ cup cold water
½ cup sugar
2 tablespoons butter
2 cups boiling water
1½ teaspoons salt
7 cups flour

Crumble the cakes of yeast in cold water and let stand a few minutes. Then, stir until dissolved. Combine sugar, butter, boiling water and salt and stir until sugar and salt dissolve. Let mixture cool. Measure 4 cups flour and sift. Add flour to wet mixture and mix thoroughly. Then add yeast and mix. Add 3 more cups flour. Knead into firm dough, as for bread. Store the dough in a covered bowl in the refrigerator. Bake as wanted.

Recipes from Mable Niven Hoffman. Mable Hoffman was very creative. When the Hoffman House no longer served as a hotel, she worked at the Vogue in Gastonia and put her special touch on the hats that were sold in that shop. (1954 Woman's Club cookbook.)

From the front door of the Hoffman Hotel, the aroma of good food welcomed guests. *Photo by author.*

Europe. They are now gone, but the museum is furnished with fine antiques of the period. Having forty-four rooms, it was home to famous judges, lawyers and political candidates during sessions of court, and it was the scene of many elegant gatherings at other times. Henry Rhyne, a grandson of A.P. Rhyne and great-grandson of Moses Rhyne, tells a story of his grandfather "being mustered from the hotel" by Union soldiers. The soldiers had already heard that Lee had surrendered, but A.P. Rhyne didn't know it. They asked him if he intended to fight any more Union soldiers, and he said, "No."[50]

North Carolina governor Zebulon B. Vance, the popular Civil War and postwar-era Democrat, is said to have come to Dallas on several occasions to give speeches on political issues and to have stayed at both the Hoffman House Hotel and the White Hotel on Courthouse Square. October 21, 1886, was one documented time and 1878 was another.[51] The town was a center of politics and a gathering place for the whole county. Beautiful gardens at the hotel were filled with jonquils, roses, lilacs and irises.[52] They made for a pleasant place for guests to walk in the afternoon and relax.

Jonas Hoffman Jr. (1820–1901) succeeded Daniel Hoffman in the ownership of the hotel with his three wives and thirteen children. Later,

Puett Hoffman, son of the third wife, owned the home. During this time, the store building beside the hotel was where, as a young man, Carl Lee Hoffman, a grandson of Jonas Hoffman Jr., was employed as a clerk.

Carriage House

131 West Main Street, Behind the Hotel

In 1991, the Daniel Stowe Carriage House was built to display the twelve horse-drawn carriages and sleighs that Mr. Stowe, a twentieth-century leader in the textile industry from Belmont, bought from an antique dealer and gave to the Gaston County Museum of Art and History. This has been a significant contribution to the museum. These carriages, with the three wagons given by local residents (the Concord wagon, Tony's ice cream wagon and the farm/freight wagon) make this collection of horse-drawn vehicles the largest in the state. They date from the 1840s to the 1980s. The oldest is the 1840 farm/freight wagon, which belonged to James Hillhouse White (1802–1883), who lived near the White and Jenkins Mill on Big Long Creek. The wagon was used 170 years ago to

The 1991 Carriage House, behind the Hoffman Hotel, houses the largest collection of horse-drawn vehicles in the state. *Photo by author.*

The Carolina & North Western Railroad Depot, built in 1901, was moved in the 1970s as part of the museum. *Photo by author.*

haul flour and cornmeal down the Old Post Stagecoach Road, which ran in front of his house, to Columbia and Charleston and to bring salt back to Gaston County. In the 1970s, the farm/freight wagon was on display at the Heritage Fair in Gastonia.

Carolina & Northwestern (C&NW) Depot

201 WEST MAIN STREET, BESIDE THE LIBRARY

Built in 1901, this depot is now part of the Gaston County Museum of Art and History. It was moved from East Church Street to West Main Street, near the museum, in 1976 to house special exhibits and art classes. The depot was saved from being demolished by L.D. Guess, who at one time was the stationmaster.[53]

Railroads were central to the textile industry's rapid rise in Gaston County during the late nineteenth century and early twentieth century. Senator James Hillhouse White secured the charter for the Lenoir and Chester Railroad (which became the C&NW and later combined with the Southern Railroad). In the late 1840s and early 1850s, the Kings Mountain Railroad was one of the pioneers in steam transportation. Kings Mountain wanted to partner with a town in North Carolina that would work with it to connect the two Carolinas by rail, but it could not find any town interested. The people of Dallas, it turned out, were very interested and stepped forward. Dallas and its leaders were early to recognize the value of the railroad. Dallas incorporated the "Dallas–Kings Mountain Mail Railway," and Senator James Hillhouse White secured the charter from the North Carolina General Assembly that would allow the train to cross the state line. This was not easy because at that time, people opposed charters for railroads leading out of the state. But he was successful in the General Assembly of 1861, and the charter was granted. According to the public notice, Edward Whitesides, Lawson Wilson, Moses H. Rhyne, Jacob Froneberger, J.F. Pegram, Samuel Jarrett, J.G. Lewis and James Hillhouse White were key players in organizing the town's contribution to the railroad:

> [The] *majority of commissioners, appointed by an act of the North Carolina General Assembly, passed at last session 1860 and 1861 of the Dallas–Kings Mountain Railway Company, met in* [the] *town of Dallas (at the courthouse)* [on the] *first day of June* [and] *on motion of J.F. Pegram appointed Samuel Jarrett treasurer, who gave bond as required by NC General Assembly. James Hillhouse White and J. Froneberger were appointed committee to ascertain amount of stock, $50,000, subscribed by for stock for the charter. On motion of* [James Hillhouse] *White, Lawson Wilson and J.G. Lewis were appointed delegates to represent our Dallas company in a meeting on 3rd June 1861 in Yorkville with Kings Mountain Railroad Company.*[54]

At the meeting in Yorkville, South Carolina senator James Hillhouse White was introduced and proposed the two railroads' joining together, with Dallas building the railroad from Dallas to the South Carolina state line and Kings Mountain building the portion from Yorkville to the North Carolina line. (They had already built the Kings Mountain to Yorkville section.) Dallas had the charter, the company, the rights of way, the agreement and the money needed to make it happen, but the Civil War interfered with the execution of the planned railroad.

There are two accounts of what happened. The annual reports of the Lenoir and Chester Railroad indicate that Yankee troops destroyed the railroad between Kings Mountain and Yorkville. The annual reports of the Carolina & Northwestern Railroad say it was the State of South Carolina that made the Kings Mountain Railroad take up its own tracks so South Carolina could use the iron in the rails for the war effort. In any case, the result was the same: the tracks were destroyed, and the Kings Mountain Railroad was no longer in business. What was left (the Dallas charter and rights of way included) combined with the Lenoir and Chester Railroad (which later became C&NW Railroad) and planned stops in Chester, Yorkville, Dallas, Lincolnton, Newton and Lenoir. The railroad later combined with the Southern Railroad. According to *Our Kin*, the road bed between Dallas and Gastonia was graded by Jonas Hoffman and two or three associates. The sixty-three miles of the Lenoir and Chester Railroad were completed from Chester, South Carolina, through Dallas, to Lincolnton, North Carolina, on February 20, 1873, and to Lenoir by 1880.[55]

The Sandifer-Friday House was built in 1903 for Robert Sandifer, a lawyer and state senator. New owners are renaming the house the Dallas West Main Manor. *Photo by author.*

Century-Old Peach Recipe That May Have Been Served in This Home

Sun-Cooked Peach Preserves

Peel peaches and to each pound of fruit add 1¼ pounds granulated sugar. Cook very fast in a porcelain kettle. Turn out into a bowl or shallow porcelain pan. Cover with muslin or cambric; set in sunny area, stirring each day, until they seem quite transparent. They retain their flavor much better this way than when cooked on a fire. Do not cook too many at a time. Put in jars, cover with paraffin to exclude the air.

From my grandmother's 1887 cookbook; no name attached to this recipe.

Sandifer-Friday House

115 West Main Street (Lot 3)

Robert Sandifer's home was built in 1903 across from Court Square. In 1893, as an attorney and state senator, Sandifer introduced a bill in the North Carolina Senate to repeal prohibition in Gaston County. After the courthouse moved to Gastonia in 1911, Mr. Sandifer made his home in Georgia, and the house was bought by Latham Friday.[56] The tin roof on this house, removed in 2011, was of special interest because it was made of square tiles called the "Dallas Shingle" and was patented in 1910 by Dallas resident Howard M. Clemmer. If you walk around town, you will notice many tin roofs on century-old homes. The roofs are real Dallas originals. They are especially noticeable on Trade and Gaston Streets. When asbestos shingles became popular, the tin-tile roofs were no longer in style and fell out of use.

The Old Dallas Grill

Corner of West Main and Gaston Streets (Lot 1)

In the 1940s and '50s, the Dallas Grill, "Home of Good Eats," was the place where the jukebox played your favorite songs and young people danced the

LUNCH AT THE DALLAS GRILL

LEMON PIE

½ cup lemon juice
1 can sweetened condensed milk
1 cup whipped evaporated milk
8-inch graham cracker pie crust, chilled
Whipped cream

Stir lemon juice into sweetened condensed milk. Fold in whipped canned milk. Pour into graham cracker crust. Chill. Just before serving, top with whipped cream.

Courtesy of the author.

PIMENTO CHEESE SANDWICHES

¾ cup mayonnaise
1 pound sharp cheddar cheese, grated (not packaged)
1 (4-ounce) jar pimentos, drained and chopped
Salt and pepper to taste

Mix mayonnaise (some people add a little cream cheese, and a few drops Worcestershire sauce as well) with grated sharp cheddar cheese, pimentos and salt and pepper. Add more mayonnaise or cheese, as needed. Mix well with a mixer. Cover and refrigerate overnight.

To make sandwiches, spread on two slices of loaf bread and press together. Butter bread and then grill sandwich until bread is toasted and cheese starts to melt. This is also sometimes used as the cheese on a cheeseburger or in a cheese omelet.

Courtesy of the author.

In 1947, the Old Dallas Grill was a gathering place for friends, food and dancing in Dallas. *Photo by author.*

swing or bop. On the wall around the red Naugahyde–covered booths were the selectors where you put in your dimes and quarters to hear your favorite music. The large jukebox was at the end of the room, and teenagers got up and danced on the floor in front of it. The "selectors" were around the room on the walls, one over each booth, and were where you selected your music and put your money if you didn't want to get up and walk to the jukebox. You could select the music from your seat or at the jukebox, and of course, there was a soda fountain. The Old Dallas Grill was the scene of many "happy days" that really happened right here on the Square. The grill opened in 1947, and my dad and I often walked from his office in the Hoffman House Hotel to the grill to get pimento cheese sandwiches. Pop Absure and Willie Ray served the best hamburgers and hot dogs anywhere around, and there was always a lemon pie on the counter. The lunch crew from Dallas High School ordered cheeseburgers with fries served by Lee Clemmer and Miss Ruth (Lineberger), who were the next proprietors. Not only did they take care of your hunger, but they also let you know that you were in pleasant company.[57]

Rhyne-Cloninger House

103 EAST MAIN STREET (LOT 21)

This home was built in 1901 and owned by Rob Rhyne and later was the home of the Paul Cloninger family. It has been said that when Rob Rhyne rode by in his car (one of the first automobiles in Dallas), everyone in town ran outside to watch. How appropriate that every year, there is an Antique Auto Show on Memorial Day weekend sponsored by the Dallas Optimist Club held here in the Dallas Historic District on Main Street beside this home. The show continues on up the street in front of the Gaston County Museum of Art and History. The museum usually has crafts, programs and food at the same time, and there are horse-drawn wagon rides around the square provided by Lewis Farm; the event is very much a street fair, too.

The very first automobile in Dallas was reported in the *Textile Review*, reprinted in the *Gazette* in 1965, to have been a little two-seater red Maxwell roadster. In May 1909, it was delivered in a crate to the C&NW depot for Fred

This home was built in 1901 and bought by Rob Rhyne and was later owned by Paul Cloninger. *Photo by author.*

Mary Jo's Pig-Pickin' Cake

Serve to friends and neighbors at a "pig pickin'," a gathering where a whole barbecued pig is the featured food. This cake is the traditional dessert.

CAKE:

1 package yellow cake mix
¾ cup oil
4 eggs
1 medium can mandarin oranges and juice (cut up)

Mix all ingredients. Prepare cake pans by greasing them and adding a little flour to the pans so the cake will come out easily. Bake in three layers at 350 degrees. Pour pineapple juice (from the can of crushed pineapple below) over cake layers while they are still warm from the oven.

FROSTING:

1 small can crushed pineapple, drained; keep the juice and put pineapple juice on warm cake
1 package instant vanilla pudding
1 large carton Cool Whip

Mix crushed pineapple, pudding and Cool Whip and spread on cake layers.

Robinson, superintendent of the Moro-Webb Mill. R.D. Beam went along to pick it up because it had to be assembled before it could be driven, and of course, neither of them had ever driven a car before. Soon a crowd gathered to give advice and watch as the wheels, fenders, brass headlights and other parts were attached. Mrs. Robinson said later that its first trip was to a Masonic picnic at High Shoals with several stops along the way to let the car cool down.

Before it was the site of the Rhyne house, this lot had a long, narrow, two-room, two-story home that faced Main Street where Grandma Morris and her daughter, Aunt Call Weathers lived. Grandma Morris was present at most of the births in Dallas during her time.[58]

One of the more well-known people of recent times to have grown up in the Rhyne-Cloninger House was Mary Jo Cloninger (1932), daughter of

Paul Cloninger. He had a barbershop, grocery store and sewing machine repair shop next door to the home. In 1951, when she was nineteen years old, Mary Jo started going to mills to buy cloth. She sold cloth that was much in demand in her father's shop. Many women still made clothes by hand for their families. Women even went with their husbands to the feed stores to pick out the sacks the feed came in because they were made of pretty, brightly colored cloth, and the women would use the cloth to make aprons. All the department stores of the time had fabric and notions sections, but Mary Jo's Cloth Store provided many more choices of beautiful cloth. People from all over the state came to Mary Jo's to shop. Many women in town worked for Mary Jo because they knew so much about cloth and sewing.

TO THE EAST OF THE SQUARE

Evon Theater

CORNER OF GASTON AND EAST MAIN (LOT 20)

This was the site of the old Evon Theater. Following World War II, movie theaters became hugely popular in Dallas. In January 1947, Dallas was blessed with the memorable Evon Theater, named for Evon Houser, who owned the property at the time and was also the editor of the *Dallas Advocate* newspaper. This theater was built about twenty years after the first all-talking movie was made, but this wasn't the first movie theater in town.

What a delight to get to go to the "Picture Show" for a Saturday afternoon matinee. Popcorn was a nickel a bag, and a box of Milk Duds would last through the whole movie. Jim McDaniel managed the theater and also resided above on the second floor. The movie house seated around 150, with tickets costing forty cents for adults and nine cents for children. Most of the movies were Bud Abbott and Lou Costella or Westerns. Double features, cartoons and newsreels were also part of the trips to the movies.

As most good things often do come to an end, so did our dear movie house. At present, the building is home to a much-needed Shelton Dry Cleaners. The small building on the right has been a laundry and a taxi stand and is now a popular pizza shop.[59]

Madge White Houser's Meatloaf

For a good supper before a movie, try this recipe.

2 pounds lean ground beef
1 large onion, minced
¾ cup bread crumbs
1 egg, beaten
1 (14-ounce) can diced tomatoes, drained and juice reserved
3 strips bacon
½ to 1 cup tomato juice (if necessary)

Mix first four ingredients and the juice from the tomatoes. Add salt and pepper to taste. Shape into loaf and place in baking pan. Lay bacon across top of loaf. Bake in a hot oven (400 degrees) until bacon browns. Remove bacon and reduce heat to 350 degrees. Cover loaf with canned tomatoes. Continue baking until done, about 1½ hours. If meatloaf becomes too dry, add more tomato juice around sides of loaf during baking period. Finish cooking the bacon and serve it on the side of the meatloaf.

1, 2, 3, 4 Cake

This is an old recipe used long ago to teach very young girls how to make cakes. They could measure out the ingredients beforehand without the recipe because they followed a numerical order: 1 cup butter, 1 cup milk, 2 teaspoons baking powder, 2 teaspoons vanilla, etc. The ingredients have been reorganized here to follow the recipe instructions.

1 cup butter, softened
2 cups sugar
4 eggs
2 teaspoons vanilla extract
3 cups flour
2 teaspoons baking powder
1 cup milk

Cream the butter and sugar. Add the eggs and vanilla. Sift the flour and baking powder together and alternate adding it and the milk to the butter mixture until well combined. Bake in a 350-degree oven for 45 minutes to 1 hour. Test with toothpick to make sure it is done.

Recipes from Madge White Houser, who was a Dallas historian and the person everyone consulted if you had a question about the history of the town. She was a "town mother."

The Evon Theater, now Shelton Cleaners, was a popular place for Saturday afternoon matinees in the 1950s. *Photo by author.*

The White House Hotel (NRHD)

116 Gaston Street (Lot 19)

There were five hotels in Dallas, with the largest two being the Hoffman House Hotel and the White House Hotel. The White House Hotel sits on Gaston Street facing the front of the courthouse. Usually, Democrats stayed at the White House Hotel and Republicans at the Hoffman House Hotel. Uriah Matthews built the White House, first called the Matthews Hotel, on lot 19, shortly after the Civil War. Originally, it had a long, two-storied ell (wing) with some dormitory-type rooms, a storeroom and kitchen to the south side (the ell has been removed) and guest rooms upstairs. The walls of the house were made of concrete using sand and cows' hair. Floors were made of wide boards held together with wooden pegs. Uriah Matthews also owned a grocery store.

Lady Baltimore Cake

Use the 1,2,3,4 Cake recipe (page 53) for the cake.

FOR FILLING:

2 cups sugar
2 cups fresh coconut
1 cup coconut milk
2 tablespoons cornstarch
½ cup orange juice
2 cups chopped walnuts
½ cup roughly chopped raisins

Put sugar, coconut and coconut milk into saucepan and boil, 3 to 4 minutes. Dissolve cornstarch in orange juice and add to saucepan. Cook until mixture falls in lumps from spoon and then remove from heat. Let stand until lukewarm. Add raisins and nuts. Spread between cake layers and on top. Then ice with 7-minute white icing.

Recipe from Iola White Martin.[60] *Iola was one of my mother's sisters.*

FOR 7-MINUTE FROSTING:

3 egg whites
¼ teaspoon cream of tartar
½ cup white Karo syrup
3 teaspoons water
⅛ teaspoon salt
1 cup sugar

Mix all ingredients in a double boiler or heatproof bowl. While cooking in double boiler (or in heatproof bowl placed on a saucepan), beat on low with mixer for 1 minute to combine ingredients. Then, beat on high for 7 minutes, or until icing stands in stiff peaks. Remove from heat. Cool slightly before putting on the cake.

Recipe from Pearl Jenkins Summey.

The White House Hotel built by Uriah Matthews, originally the Matthews Hotel, is part of the Dallas Historic District. *Photo by author.*

In 1900, John Blair White, a Civil War veteran, clerk of superior court in Gaston County from 1878 to 1890, member of the North Carolina House of Representatives (1893) and one of James Hillhouse White's twelve children, bought the hotel and ran it. John White's married daughter, Madge White Houser, returned to Dallas with her husband in 1898 and lived much of her life here. My mother's family (her father was a nephew of John White) lived here for a time after her family moved to town from the farm. She attended high school at the old Gaston College. Earlier, the hotel had had many boarders who were students at the college. The White House Hotel was the scene of many grand college graduation parties and receptions.

One of my mother's sisters, Iola White Martin, met her future husband while she was living in the White House Hotel. Everett Martin was a supervisor for a crew of workers who were building the railroad through Gaston County, and he boarded at the White House Hotel. After they were married, the Martins lived in Fitzgerald, Georgia. One of the White family's favorite party desserts was Lady Baltimore Cake, served at many of the receptions at this hotel.

The Friday Home

128 Gaston Street (Lot 18)

Originally, this house was called the "old store house." It was built up to the street in the middle of the 1800s. Shortly after the war, Captain J.I. Holland bought the store and added one room to the downstairs and two rooms to the upstairs. Later, the house was occupied by two other men, Charlie Hoffman and R.J. Durham. After each of the men lived in the house for several years, it was sold to Noah Alexander. Alexander sold the house to the Friday family, a very talented family: Latham Friday was a mayor of Dallas, Beth Friday was the first woman in Dallas to run for public office and their children all did well. Their youngest son, John Friday, was a highly respected judge. The house was moved back from the sidewalk, and a great deal of remodeling was done. The walls are made of pine, and under the floor are still the logs and wooden pegs used for nails when the house was first built. The house contains a double floor. Mrs. Friday added many antiques, which made the home even more beautiful.[61]

Beth Friday's Date-Nut Bread

This was a favorite food served in this home.

2 tablespoon butter
1 cup sugar
1 cup dates, chopped
1 cup boiling water
1 beaten egg
2 cups flour
1 teaspoon baking soda
½ cup chopped pecans

Combine the butter, sugar and dates in a mixing bowl. Pour in boiling water and cool. Add the remaining ingredients to form dough. Bake 1 hour in moderate 350-degree oven.

The Friday House was the boyhood home of William C. Friday. *Photo by author.*

On March 29, 1957, William C. Friday, president of the University of North Carolina (from 1956 to 1986), gave an address on the Court Square of the town of Dallas.[62] It was the occasion of the unveiling of the North Carolina historical highway marker for the town of Dallas that was placed on the Square near Trade Street. It reads, "Dallas, Named for G.M. Dallas, first county seat of Gaston County 1846–1911; Site of Gaston College, now extinct, Courthouse built in 1848 is here."[63] The marker was unveiled by Gale White and Gail Houser, great-great-granddaughters of James Hillhouse White, one of the principal founders of the county. At the same ceremony, Jane Holland, daughter of Mr. and Mrs. Claudius Holland Jr. and Gary Holland, son of Mr. and Mrs. Sam A.R. Holland, unveiled the plaque on the boulder in front of the courthouse honoring Jesse Holland for his role in granting land for the town. On that day, Dr. Friday, one of the youngest university presidents in America, stood facing the Old Gaston County Courthouse surrounded by neighbors and friends and then turned to look across Gaston Street to this home where he grew up. Dr. Friday was the son of Beth and Latham Friday. In his speech, he said, "Let us dedicate ourselves out of gratitude to the better

WILLIAM C. FRIDAY (1920–2012)

On March 29, 1957, William C. Friday, age thirty-six, was one of the youngest university presidents in America. Pictured in front of the courthouse are Dr. Friday, speaking; seated on the left, Beth Friday, Dr. Friday's mother; and Maria Pasour, chairwoman of the committee for the unveiling of the markers ceremony. On the right are Mrs. Spargo, Dora Rhodes Carpenter and Reverend Huggins. Standing behind are Kitty Kay Thornburg, Barbara Carpenter, Elizabeth Carpenter, Gail Houser and Gale White. *Courtesy of Mary Ann Friday Carpenter.*

This was the boyhood home of William C. Friday, born in Raphine, Virginia, in 1920. Bill was one of five children of Beth and Latham Friday. In school, he was a debater, played baseball and basketball and wrote sports columns for the *Gastonia Gazette*. One of the people in town once jokingly said that if he had stayed with baseball, he might have amounted to something, but he was destined for greater things. He graduated from high school in a class of twelve as president of his class. He went to Wake Forest and then to North Carolina State, where he graduated, again as president of his class. Bill married Ida Howell. When he joined the U.S. Navy, where he was a lieutenant during World War II, he observed that the African American soldiers were usually assigned the most dangerous tasks. From then on, during his life, he tried to effect change for the better wherever he went. He had a knack for understanding people and could relate to anyone. After the navy, he enrolled in UNC's Law School, where he was president of the Law School Association and graduated in a class that included William Aycock (future governor), Terry Sanford (future governor) and Dickson Phillips (future Federal Court of Appeals judge and college professor). Following law school, he became dean of students at UNC and then secretary of the university. At the age of thirty-five, he was elected president of the University of North Carolina, a position he held for thirty years, the longest-serving president in the university's history. As president, he defended academic freedom and worked for the repeal of the 1963 Speaker Ban Law. He was a member of the Carnegie Commission on Higher Education, and that work resulted in the Higher Education Act of 1965 and the creation of Pell Grants, which make it possible for many undergraduates to attend college. He felt that a good education should be available to anyone willing to study hard for it regardless of his or her economic condition. With increasing enrollments, he recommended the expansion of the university. When the university combined its schools, he was chosen president of the sixteen-campus University of North Carolina. He was cofounder of the Knight Commission on intercollegiate athletics, which worked for integrity in sports; chaired commissions on poverty and literacy for two North Carolina governors; helped create the White House Fellows Program and the Research Triangle; and received the North Carolina Award, the state's highest honor. He held more than twenty honorary degrees, and both he and Ida received the North Carolina General Assembly's Order of the Long Leaf Pine Award in a special session. The Council for the Advancement and Support of Education ranked him as the nation's most effective university president. He died on October 12, 2012, the 219th anniversary of the laying of the cornerstone of the first building of the University of North Carolina at Chapel Hill. Dallas has not forgotten Bill Friday's example.

ways of life, and with God's help, we can move ahead to even greater progress in the future." In this state, Dr. Friday is known for his many contributions to North Carolina and higher education.

The 1957 Educational Heritage Centennial Pageant written by Allie White Hoffman and directed by Sam Phillips, both teachers in Dallas, celebrated Teacher Institutes. The play was presented on the same day Dr. Friday gave the March 29 speech on the Court Square.

Rhyne Store (NRHD)

130–132 NORTH GASTON STREET (LOT 17)

The two-story, handmade-brick Rhyne Store is the oldest business building in Dallas. It was built in 1850 as a general store, and Moses Rhyne, the

When the courthouse burned in 1874, the court met in the Rhyne Store, built by Moses Rhyne in 1850. *Photo by author.*

owner, lived upstairs. His wife, Margaret Hoffman Rhyne, was the daughter of Daniel Hoffman. Moses Rhyne was very active in the town and county and was a promoter of one of the first cotton mills in Gaston County. He also was a benefactor of old Gaston College. His sons, Abel P. "A.P." Rhyne and Daniel E. Rhyne, followed in their father's footsteps in the textile industry as well as in education, where both sons were leaders. Daniel E. Rhyne was the Rhyne for whom Lenoir-Rhyne University was named and was said to have bought the first automobile in North Carolina.[64] At one time, the Rhyne Store was used as a post office. In 1874, when the courthouse across the street burned and was being rebuilt, this store served as the temporary courthouse for the county. Today, it houses an antique and gift shop, The Rusty Relic, named the best antique shop in Gaston County by the *Gaston Gazette*.

Moses Rhyne and Fred D. Hoffman had an earlier general store near Tuckaseege Ford, which played an important role as a political gathering place and in the formation of the county. *The Annals of Lincoln County* records that:

James Hillhouse White (member of the House of Commons) was the first to come forth with the idea that the lower regiment of Lincoln County be separated and formed into a new county. On June 4, 1842, a group of the Lower Regiments (foremost regiments) met at the store owned by Moses H. Rhyne and Fred D. Hoffman about a mile west of Tuckaseege Ford (in what is now Mount Holly). White was there to preside and speak. He spoke earnestly and persuasively with the group and they voted not to support any candidate for the Legislature who was not outspoken in favour of dividing Lincoln County.[65]

James H. White, the incumbent, was reelected from Lincoln County to the North Carolina House of Commons in 1842 and served in the North Carolina legislature during sixteen of the next twenty years, covering the formation of Gaston County and the Civil War period. In 1842, Larkin Stowe was elected to the North Carolina Senate, and Richard Rankin joined them in 1844 in the House of Commons. These men worked together to get the bill passed in the house on December 2 and in the senate on December 5, and it became law on December 21, 1846. This was the act of the legislature that made Gaston County a county.

Jesse Holland House
406 East Trade Street

This historic old house, "east of the Court Square, across the tracks on the north bank of Trade Street," was built in 1848 on land thought to be granted to Andrew Holland (pioneer) in a March 24, 1755 patent of 350 acres on Long Creek. Andrew Holland came to Dallas in 1735.[66] This house was built as the town of Dallas was being laid out and is what remains of the oldest house in Dallas. The original home was a two-story handmade-brick house with a full front porch and a two-door entrance built in the Dutch style with curved arches over the doors. It was the fifth brick house built in Gaston County. (Toward the end of the twentieth century, drastic alterations were made to the house, and the second story and porch were removed.) Before this house was built, Jesse Holland (1786–1856), the son of Julius Holland and Mary Gaston Holland, lived in his father's house, two hundred yards from Long Creek Baptist Church, where Julius was the minister.

Jesse married Martha Jane Hanks, daughter of Richard "Dicky" Hanks, who claimed he was the uncle of Nancy Hanks, mother of President Abraham

Southern Corn Bread

2 eggs
2½ cups buttermilk
1 teaspoon baking soda
1 teaspoon salt
2 tablespoons lard, melted
1 pint cornmeal, sifted and scalded with 1 cup hot water

Beat eggs. Add buttermilk, baking soda, salt and melted lard. Add cornmeal. Stir well. Pour into a well-greased pan. Bake in a quick oven. One tablespoon of sugar may be added. (Served in early homes with homemade sorghum molasses for sopping as a dessert.)

Jesse Holland's "new" house was built in 1848 as the town of Dallas was being laid out. *Photo by author.*

Lincoln. Nancy lived with her uncle's family in what is now Belmont for several years.[67] Jesse Holland, as mentioned previously, was active in the movement to establish Gaston County and sold the land for the courthouse, the jail, the four churches and the land for the town of Dallas, which was the county seat for the newly formed Gaston County. On February 3, 1847, the first governing court was organized and held in Jesse Holland's house near Long Creek Baptist Church.[68]

The first Gaston County officials, appointed on February 3, 1847, included the following:

Justices (moved over to Gaston County because they now lived in the newly created county):[69] Isaac Holland (chairman), Alfred Abernathy, Andrew Love, Andrew Hoyle, Jacob Plonk, John Webster, James Ferguson, R.M. Alexander, Abram Mauney, Thos. P. McGill, Robert Johnston, John Oates, William J. Wilson, John McGinnis, Major Whitesides, J.C. Hand, John Falls, Andrew B. Cox. Milton A. Smith, John G. Lewis, A.W. Davenport, Milton A. Smith, (newly appointed) Christian Eaker, John R. Cates, Richard Rankin, Alexander Waar and James M. Hannah.
Clerk of Court: John H. Roberts
Sheriff: Benjamin Morris
Registrar for County: James Ferguson
County Trustee: Richard Rankin
Gaston County Commissioners: William J. Wilson, Larkin Stowe and James Hillhouse White

Claudius Holland House

128 East Trade Street (Lot 38)

This home belonged to Claudius Daniel Holland, son of Ephraim Holland and grandson of Jesse Holland. Claudius was a graduate of West Point, an attorney in Dallas and Gastonia and a mayor of Dallas. The house was built on the former site of Ephraim Holland's doctor's office and between where Ephraim's home once stood and the county jail.

Ephraim Holland (1831–1896) was the first doctor born in Gaston County. He graduated from the National Medical College in Washington, D.C. During the Civil War, Ephraim served the Confederate cause as an army surgeon for North Carolina and was in charge of the Military Hospital

Persimmon Pudding

1 quart water
2 quarts persimmons
1 quart sweet milk
2 cups sugar
1 teaspoon cinnamon
½ teaspoon vanilla extract
½ teaspoon ground ginger
½ teaspoon salt
3 tablespoons butter, melted
1 quart sweet potatoes, grated
2 cups bread crumbs
2 eggs, beaten separately
½ teaspoon baking soda
1 teaspoon baking powder
3 cups flour

Put water over persimmons and run through colander. Add sweet milk, sugar, cinnamon, vanilla, ginger, salt, melted butter, grated sweet potatoes, bread crumbs, eggs, baking soda, baking powder and flour. Mix well and bake in moderate oven (350 degrees) for about 1 hour.

Old-Fashioned Coconut Pie

1 coconut (small), grated
3 tablespoon sugar
2 tablespoon orange juice or coconut milk flavored with ½ teaspoon vanilla
2 eggs
¾ cup milk or a mixture of leftover coconut milk and sweet milk

Combine all the ingredients. Put into a pie shell and bake until filling is set and pie is done, about 45 minutes.

This was the home of Claudius Holland, a grandson of Jesse Holland, who was an attorney and mayor of Dallas. *Photo by author.*

Number 8 in Raleigh. He married Julia Courts, the daughter of Daniel Courts, the state treasurer of North Carolina. After the war, Ephraim and his wife came back home to Dallas. They bought the old Farmers' Hotel, which had been built by Johnny Smith around 1850, and remodeled it for their home. The house became known for its beautiful boxwoods, shrubs and flowering trees; however, the home no longer stands.[70]

On September 5, 1887, twelve doctors met in Dallas at the office of Dr. J.H. Jenkins to form the county's first medical and surgical society. Dr. Ephriam B. Holland was elected the president, Dr. I. Blair Hunter was the vice-president and Dr. John H. Jenkins was the secretary-treasurer. In 1894, a typhoid epidemic hit the county. Tommy Henderson, a young clerk in J.R. Lewis's general store, came down with a deadly case of the fever. All treatments of the day were tried and failed. Everyone had given up hope. Dr. Jenkins decided to try a blood transfusion, but there were no human donors. As a last resort, he decided to use fresh lamb's blood instead, and it was successful. The operation took place in the parlor of the Rhyne house on Trade Street, which is the large red house across the street from the Dallas Baptist Church. Mary Modina Lewis held the lamp for Dr. Jenkins. Henderson responded and recovered.[71]

Dr. Ephraim and Julia Courts Holland were buried in the old Dallas Presbyterian cemetery on South College Street.

The Old Gaston County Jail (NRHD)

108 EAST TRADE STREET (LOT 37)

Built in 1847, this two-story handmade-brick building was Gaston County's first jail. There were four rooms on each floor with the jailer's family's residence on the first floor, and the prisoners confined to cells on the second floor. Each of the small windows had iron bars across it. The handmade bricks were made on site, directly behind the jail.

There is a story told by my grandmother Edna Pasour White (1877–1967) about the jail, which follows:

The old Gaston County jail, built by Abraham Mauney in 1847, is part of the Dallas Historic District. *Photo by author.*

HILDA'S OLD-FASHIONED TEA CAKES

1 stick (½ cup) margarine or butter
1 egg
1 cup sugar
2 tablespoons milk
½ teaspoon vanilla
1¾ cups self-rising flour

Cream first five ingredients. Add flour and mix until well blended. Chill the dough about twenty minutes, cut the cakes with a round cookie cutter or cut into squares. Bake for eight minutes at 375 degrees.

> *In the winter of 1887, I was spending the night with some of my relatives whose father was the jailer at the time. Late in the night, a group of men came knocking on the door of the jail demanding a certain prisoner. The jailer refused, so they pulled their guns and took the prisoner.* [Edna remembered hearing the chains around the prisoner's ankles, rattling down the stone steps from the second-floor cell.] *He was led down to a tree on the Lower Dallas Road* [New Hope Road] *near Big Long Creek and they hung* [sic] *him there.*[72]

(In 1965, the *Charlotte Observer* interviewed her and quoted her story, the same story she told us.)

Hilda Stowe Queen told me when she and her brother, Dalton Stowe (Dallas historian and historical society charter member), were young, after the courthouse and jail had been moved to Gastonia, in 1931 they lived with their parents in an apartment on the first floor of the old jail. They paid seven dollars a month for rent. From her bed, she could hear Gaston Street being paved. It was the first paved street in Gaston County. During the day, children in town played with the rocks in the street. Early automobiles in Dallas—Ray Rhyne's and Fred Robinson's were two of the first in 1909—went "bump, bump" as they fell off the pavement onto the dirt road of Trade Street. Later, she could hear the noise from the Dallas-Stanley Road as it was being paved at night. Workers only paved one side of that road, because, after all, "you could only use one side at a time."[73]

To the North of the Square

The Merchants on Trade Street

Looking west, from Trade and Gaston, the white building (Lot 11) in the background was the 1904 bank and later, in 1957, a post office. The bank was one of the many that failed during the stock market crash of 1929. In the center (Lot 13), the largest building is the Setzer General Store (NRHD) was built in 1870, and it and the Rhyne Store on Gaston Street, built 1850, are the two oldest business buildings in town. The Setzer building was originally three stories high, but the top floor was removed. Mary Jo's Cloth Store, the newer building (Lot 15) in the foreground, was built in the 1960s. Now, its architecture, too, is becoming a classic of its era, and in some places, similar buildings have the historic designation.

Between the 1940s and 1960s, there were grocery stores with long poles and hooks to reach items on the top shelves (Brady Ratchford had such a store on the corner of Gaston and Church Streets), Summey's Drug Store with a busy soda fountain where you could stop by for lunch, Lee Clemmer's Alex doughnuts hot from the oven, Miss Ruth's Pie Company with pecan pies and coconut pies, Pasours' Clothing Store, Friday and Hovis Barber Shop, Henry Stroup's Barber Shop, George Rhyne's thread repair shop, Frances's Dress Shop, Carlton Cloninger's Grocery Store on Gaston Street, Summey and Jenkins Hardware Store, Rudisill Brothers Tin Shop, the Ingle's American Textile Sheet Metal Works, A.P.H. Rhyne Grocery Store, Fordham's Nursery, Tom Summey's Grocery Store, a watch repair shop, Clyde Ratchford's Bus Service going through town, Dr. Will's office, Ratchford Clothing Store and many other businesses around Dallas. Now, most of these are gone, and there are other names, such as Dallas Paint Store, Courtney's, Edward Jones Investments, Ideal Upholstry, Ratchford's Tire Service, Shelton Dry Cleaners, Papa's Pizza, Bank of America, Branch Banking and Trust Company, Ingles Grocery Store and Food Lion, doctors' offices, dentists, auto repair shops, grocery stores, beauty shops, antique shops, restaurants, and coffee shops.

The Setzer building, located in the middle of this block on Trade Street, is part of the Dallas Historic District. *Photo by author.*

I can remember when the Harlem Globe Trotters made a stop at the Dallas gym to give us a basketball performance we've never forgotten to the tune of "Sweet Georgia Brown." That wasn't the only type of basketball games we had. At least once a year, we would have Donkey Basketball, where all the players rode donkeys. The games took place in the Dallas gym. Another memory some folks still talk about is the day Bob Summey (future Baptist minister) took a dare. He stood out on Trade Street and threw a baseball over the courthouse to the Hoffman House Hotel on Main Street. They said he couldn't do it, but he did. Many also remember the days "Sweet Daddy Grace," Bishop Charles Manuel Grace from Cape Verde, Africa, who started the House of Prayer for All People would come through Dallas in a big parade.

The earliest memories are some of the strangest, however. Carrie Puett Lewis wrote of an organ grinder with a monkey doing tricks for money, a man who went up and down Gaston and Trade Streets with a dancing bear and a man and a cart who came by to sharpen knives. There were washerwomen who went from house to house with big wash tubs to wash clothes. She also told of medicine men with snake oil standing on boxes and making speeches to anyone who would listen. Of course, people gathered to watch.[74] Clarence Thornburg (1898–1989) told of Buffalo Bill's Wild West Show.[75] Most everyone went to see the performers ride and shoot when they came through.

To the West of the Square

The Town Clock, Trade Street

The town clock on the corner of Trade and Holland Streets was given by David Cloninger in memory of his father, Carlton Cloninger, and in honor of his mother, Coleen Cloninger, both of whom, at different times, served as mayors of Dallas. Coleen Cloninger was the first female mayor in Gaston County, elected in 1992.

Dallas was a planned town. The county seat was put in the center of the county to make it more accessible to the people it served and to solve the problem of the county seat at Lincolnton being so far away and difficult to get to by buggy. Most of the main roads ran through Dallas. In a 1992 article, the *Gaston Gazette* interviewed Coleen Cloninger and quoted Lamar Stroup, owner of the Dallas Paint Center, as saying, "I really think everybody in Gaston County who starts out to go somewhere comes through

The Dallas town clock was given in memory of Carlton Cloninger and in honor of Coleen Cloninger, two mayors of Dallas. *Photo by author.*

Dallas," and that is exactly as it was intended in 1848. Those first three county commissioners—Wilson, Stowe and White—with Andrew Love, the treasurer of public buildings, were asked to select the spot for and contract and supervise the building of a courthouse and jail within two miles of Long Creek Baptist Church, and the roads went through Dallas so it would be easy to get to the courthouse from all over the county.[76]

Early mayors included Eli Pasour, who was the first mayor of Dallas, as well as Lee Wilson, Fred Pasour, Claudius Holland, William L. Sherrill, J.W. Summey, Robert Rhyne, Latham Friday, Fred Robinson, Blair Falls Houser, Puett Hoffman, Evon Houser, Dr. W.W. Latham, S.A. Wilkins, J.C. Puett, A.J. Maxwell, K.F. Lineberger, W.W. Fogle, Polie Cloninger, David Hoyle (who became state senator), Carlton Cloninger, Coleen Cloninger and Rick Coleman.

PEANUT BRITTLE

This is a good, old-fashioned treat. Bill Friday made it every Christmas and gave it to his friends.[77]

2 cups sugar
1 cup Karo syrup
½ cup water
4 cups raw peanuts
1 tablespoon baking soda
½ teaspoon salt

Mix the sugar and syrup with the water and bring them to a boil; then add the raw peanuts. Cook slowly until peanuts are parched. Add the baking soda, stirring continuously. Add the salt and stir to dissolve. Pour on greased marble slab to cool and harden. Break in pieces. Put in tightly covered jar.

Recipe from Carrie Puett Lewis who was the historian for the Woman's Club for many years and wrote for the Gaston County Historical Society Bulletin.

Lewis Mill Office

117 North Holland Street (Lot 9)

This building was built by R.S. Lewis in 1904. Mr. Lewis was the secretary-treasurer of Morowebb Mill in Dallas, and he first used this building as his office. Later, when he was a postmaster, the building was used as an early post office. It has had many different uses in town. Today, it is owned by Larry and Wayne Ann Clemmer Penley of Penley Associates. Their son, Larry Penley Jr.—who was born in 1959 and grew up in Dallas, attending William C. Friday Middle School and North Gaston High School and then Clemson University—has made a name for himself in the golf world. After playing pro golf, he coached at Clemson and became the first coach in the history of college golf to take a Division I team to the NCAA Regional and then to the NCAA Championship in the same year. He was named National Coach of the Year in 2003 and inducted into the College Golf Hall of Fame in 2004 at the age of forty-four, one of the youngest on record.

R.S. Lewis used his Morowebb Mill Office when he was the mill's secretary-treasurer. *Photo by author.*

Smyre-Pasour House (NRHD)
113–115 NORTH HOLLAND STREET (LOT 8)

This home, built in 1850, is considered a landmark in Dallas. It was first owned by Dr. J.F. Smyre and, a year later, was sold to Eli Pasour, who became postmaster in 1868 (Dallas's sixth) and again in 1889. His wife, Catherine, was postmistress in 1880. Eli served one term in the state legislature in 1881 and was elected the first mayor of Dallas. Eli Pasour was an only child. His father died

The Smyre-Pasour House, a Dallas landmark built in 1850, is one of the oldest residences in town. *Photo by author.*

L.A. and Lizzie Costner Thornburg's home (Lot 7) with his children's families gathered for a reunion in 1927. They are seated by family (left to right): Mamie Thornburg Rhodes's family, Blanche Thornburg Carpenter's family, Martha Thornburg Pasour's family, Win S. Thornburg's family and D. S. Thornburg's family. *Courtesy of the Thornburg family.*

Herselia's Coffee for Fifty

1 pound ground coffee
6 to 8 quarts cold water

Put coffee into a muslin bag in a large kettle. Add water and let stand several hours. Bring to boil and simmer 3 minutes.

at the age of twenty-five and his mother, Elizabeth Rhyne Pasour, remarried one of the Linebergers. The family spent the war years at Woodlawn Mill.

Around 1870, part of this home was used as a school by Herselia Pasour Costner, one of Eli and Catherine Rhodes Pasour's daughters, who taught private school in the home. It was the second school in Dallas. Some of the students were Alice Hoffman Rhodes, Annie and Alethea Pasour, Will Hoffman, Claudius Holland and Laban Jenkins. Alethea Pasour, a sister of Herselia, was a clerk for the post office when her father was postmaster and then continued in the post office for many years. An earlier pre–Civil War one-room school was near where the old broom factory stood on North College Street. O.C. Odell taught school there. In 1881, Mr. Odell was the county superintendent of schools.

Some of the old homes now missing from the square, according to the Historical Society Bulletin from May 1967, include the following:

Lot 7: L.A. Thornburg's second home shared with his second wife, Lizzy Costner.[78]

Lot 1: The home of Winchester and Mary Stowe Pegram was built in the late 1850s. Colonel Morris built this home, which stood on the corner lot for almost one hundred years. It was said to have been the first home built on the Square and was a beautiful home made almost entirely of heart pine that probably could have lasted much longer.

Lot 2: The Wilson-Spargo home built before 1898 and damaged by fire in 1980 had a second-floor cantilevered porch. This home was on the National Register of Historic Places before it burned.

Lot 15: The Tavern Hotel built by Andrew Hoyle around 1850 was the second house to be built on the original land track. The Winchester Pegrams ran that hotel.

Lot across Holland Street, west of the bank, on the corner of Holland and Trade Streets: The home of James Robert and Barbara A. Katherine Lineberger Lewis; a double porch identified this home.

Lot 11: The Froneberger home was said to have been on Lot 11 before the white bank building was built.

Roberts-Lewis House

109 NORTH HOLLAND STREET (LOT 6)

This home is one of the oldest in Dallas. It is located on the southwest corner of Court Square and was built in 1852 for John Roberts, the first clerk of court for Gaston County. Many different families have lived here—Beatys, Hollands, Rudisills, Lohrs and others—but for one hundred years, it has been owned by descendants of Robert Lewis. Carrie Lewis noted in her article in the *Gaston County Historical Society Bulletin* in 1967 that the porch of this home usually had many red geraniums on the steps and roses in the yard.

Built in 1852 for John Roberts, the first clerk of court of Gaston County, this home has had many owners. *Photo by author.*

6
AROUND AND ABOUT TOWN

Churches, Educational Institutions and Homes in the Neighborhood

Churches

Presbyterian Church of Dallas (Cemetery)
Corner of Church and College (Lot 76)

The old Presbyterian Church of Dallas was erected here in 1851 by Andrew Hoyle and was dedicated on July 15, 1851. The cemetery is still here and has the graves of the Hollands, Puetts, Rhynes, Pegrams, Fronebergers, Fridays, Pasours and other early pioneer families. This church was where my mother's family and her grandparents attended, but her family is buried in the White and Jenkins Cemetery in Costner Community, a family cemetery. That was true of many people who preferred to be buried with their families in family cemeteries. Wilma Ratchford Craig, editor of the *Gaston County Historical Society Bulletin*, says there are about one hundred old family cemeteries in Gaston County. Back at the beginning of the town, the county court assigned a committee to give lots for the churches in town. This was the original corner lot for this church of twelve charter members. At his death in 1857, Andrew Hoyle's will stated, "I will that my executors shall pay to the churches of Goshen Presbyterian and Dallas Presbyterian $15 per annum to each church for six years as stipend for the ministry at those

IRISH SODA BREAD

4 cups plain flour, unsifted
1 tablespoon sugar
1 teaspoon salt
1 ½ teaspoons (level) baking soda
1 teaspoon (heaping) baking powder
Mix above well and cream with:
¾ stick soft margarine
1 cup seedless raisins
1 ½ cups buttermilk

Mix well with spatula. Turn out on floured board. Knead 20 times. Form in round bun. Place bun in greased round pie plate.

Score top with a long cross over top, using sharp knife (cut shallow cross). Bake at 350 degrees for about 1 hour. Good with coffee or tea.

Recipe from Dora Rhodes Carpenter. Dora Rhodes Carpenter was a demanding teacher of math in Dallas High School and "Aunt Dodie" to this family. Her family home, the Puett-Rhodes house, no longer exists at 803 Main. My brother, Clarence Thornburg Jr., spoke highly of her and considered her one of his great teachers. This was high praise because he received his PhD in nuclear physics from MIT in 1966.

places providing that they stay Presbyterian."[79] The first pastor was R.N. Davis. Most of the early pioneers were very religious. Many had left their homeland because of religious persecution, so the church was the center of their social lives, as well as of their spiritual lives.

The second minister, and first full-time minister, lived in Lincoln County on Morrison Road at Cottage Home, near present-day Highways 16 and 73, and "commuted" to Dallas for monthly church services. He was Dr. Robert Hall Morrison, the founder and first president of Davidson College and the father-in-law of three Confederate generals: Daniel Harvey Hill, Thomas J. "Stonewall" Jackson and Rufus Barringer. A fourth son-in-law, Alphonso Avery, was a judge in Morganton, and on occasion (March 1886 was one such time), he presided over trials in the Gaston County

The Presbyterian Church of Dallas was built by Andrew Hoyle in 1851; only the cemetery remains at this site. *Photo by author.*

Courthouse in Dallas. Anna and Thomas Jackson were married at Cottage Home in 1857 after Dr. Morrison served this church in 1854–55. In 1886, a wall in the church was cracked during an earthquake in Charleston, South Carolina. Antioch Lutheran Church also had a wall crack during the same earthquake.

First Presbyterian Church

West Trade Street

The First Presbyterian Church on West Trade Street was built in 1950 by Clarence Thornburg. It is the same church as the old Presbyterian Church of Dallas that once stood on the corner of Church and College Streets. It just has a new name, location and building.

When the Presbyterian Church of Dallas moved to Trade Street, it changed its name to First Presbyterian Church. *Photo by author.*

Holy Communion Lutheran

CORNER OF CHURCH AND GASTON (LOT 81)

The contemporary building was dedicated in 1972; however, the church has a long history with Reverend M.L. Little as the first pastor. It began in 1885 as College Chapel Church with members meeting in old Gaston College. When the college closed in 1905, a church was built one block west of the college on this corner lot and stood for sixty-five years. This is the original lot from the Jesse Holland land set aside for the Lutheran Church. In 1906, Dallas invited the United Lutheran Synod of the South (whose choice was between going to Savannah or coming to Dallas for their meetings; they decided on Dallas) to hold its meetings at Holy Communion, and the citizens of Dallas graciously provided meals and lodging in their homes for the delegates and visitors. Today, the church serves with worship, music, community concerts and social ministry. The Rhyne Family National Reunion has been held here. The whole town joins in every year to put on a chicken 'n dumpling supper in the fellowship hall to raise money for the food bank.

SOUTHERN CHICKEN 'N DUMPLINGS

This recipe was used one hundred years ago at Holy Communion Lutheran Church for community chicken 'n dumpling suppers. It was one of Beulah Brown Rhyne's recipes, and it is good. Before school cafeterias and lunchrooms, children carried their lunch, often leftovers, to school, usually in a sack or paper bag. Carl Lee Hoffman remembered taking leftover chicken 'n dumplings for his lunch, carrying them in his pocket.[80]

3 eggs
1 tablespoon lard
1 teaspoon salt
*¾ cup hot rich chicken stock**
Enough flour for stiff dough

Beat eggs and add salt. Put lard in hot stock. Add alternately ¼ cup stock and ¾ cup flour to egg mixture, beating after each until a stiff dough is formed. Roll thin (⅛ inch) and let dumplings stand in cool room on a floured cloth for 1 hour to dry. Cut dumplings in strips. Drop into boiling homemade chicken stock, stirring often. Stock should have many pieces of chicken in it from the stewed chicken. After all dumplings are in the pot, cover and let simmer on low for 30 minutes. Add more stock as needed. (Country ham bone dumplings are made this way, too. Just use a ham bone that still has some ham on it to make your stock.)

*The traditional way to make the stock is just to stew a chicken and use it for your stock and the chicken meat for the chicken 'n dumplings. If you don't want to stew a whole chicken, an easy way to make chicken stock is to use your slow cooker and add the boney parts of the chicken (backs, wings, necks that have the chicken meat and skin still attached—about half meat and half bones is good). Add two cans of chicken broth, and if you don't have a lot of boney chicken parts, add more. Then add about six or seven cups of water (enough to cover the bones), the scrap pieces or ends of carrots, celery and onions and salt and pepper. Bring to a boil and let simmer for several hours. Strain the stock, take the stewed chicken meat off the bones and add to the stock. Throw away the bones and scraps. Use stock and chicken to make your chicken 'n dumplings. Alternatively, you can just use store-bought stock.

Holy Communion Lutheran Church began as College Chapel Church in 1885 with M.L. Little as its first minister. *Photo by author.*

When Carl White Hoffman, son of Carl Lee Hoffman, a young doctor who grew up in this church, was in the United States Army in Korea, he and two assistants began giving medical aid to ninety-four children in a nearby orphanage and to the village people. They became especially interested in a young boy, Lee, whose leg had become infected with tuberculosis. Carl wrote to his mother and told her that if the Lutheran Church Women's group wanted to help someone, now was the time. The LCW was happy to send money for this cause, and with this gift and money from the fellow soldiers, the boy was able to receive treatment at the Seoul National University Hospital. Nine years later, Carl was at a Medical Convention in California where he met a fellow he had known in Korea who told him that the little boy with the diseased leg had been healed and was now leading a normal life. People receiving medical care is an everyday happening for which we are thankful, but when we send money to another land, we don't always hear the outcome. The little boy from the hut covered with rice stems in Seoul, Korea, was made well, and the LCW of Holy Communion had a part.

Dallas Baptist Church

WEST TRADE STREET

The Dallas Baptist Church is located on the corner of Trade and Maple Streets, the lot given to it by the town commissioners. It began in the 1880s with J.H. Booth as the first pastor. This church building was built in 1914. The first organ was given in 1946 by Mr. and Mrs. Lawrence Holland in

Dallas Baptist Church was built in the 1880s on its original Dallas lot. *Photo by author.*

memory of one of their sons, Larry Jr., who died during World War II and is buried in Arlington Cemetery in Virginia. In the 1940s, the four old churches (Presbyterian, Baptist, Methodist and Lutheran) each had a huge evergreen tree in its front yard. These trees were decorated with as many electric Christmas tree lights as possible and looked beautiful to everyone coming to town. Not one of the trees remains.

First Baptist Church
SOUTH RHYNE STREET

Shortly after 1876, the African American church members who had once worshiped in the balcony at Long Creek Baptist Church withdrew their membership and started the first black church in Dallas. The other churches had been given a lot on which to build a church out of the original tract of Jesse Holland land. Robert Holland, Jesse's oldest son, gave this church land on Rhyne Street, the same lot this church is on today. Reverend C.F. Gingles was an early minister at the church.

The first African American church in Dallas was First Baptist Church. *Photo by author.*

First United Methodist Church held services in the courthouse during the 1850s. *Photo by author.*

First United Methodist Church

West Main Street

The First United Methodist Church held classes in the old courthouse in the 1850s. Methodist itinerant ministers would stop there to hold services. In 1867, the faithful met at the courthouse to form a church with Reverend C.E. Land as the first minister. The corner lot offered by Jesse Holland was thought to have been at the corner of Church and Oakland, in the area near where the police station is now. The church built a wooden structure and later moved to the present location. Since they didn't have enough money to build a new church, in a show of faith, they bought the brick and had it delivered to the new site anyway.

Educational Institutions

Old Gaston College

200 Block of South College Street
(Lot 75 and five-acre campus)

A landmark in its time, old Gaston College and Gaston Female College, built in 1879, attracted students from six different states and was well known over the Carolinas for its music, art and foreign language studies. Professor Marcus Lafayette Little came to Dallas in 1882 as principal of Dallas School, sometimes called Gaston Academy. He was a Lutheran minister and believed in education and missions. He was the first minister at College Chapel Church, now Holy Communion Lutheran Church, which met in the chapel at old Gaston College. He also served some of the other Lutheran churches in the area. The school had two departments, a primary one and a higher prep school and college department. By 1886, there were six departments: Preparatory, Normal, Collegiate, Musical, Art and Commerce. The higher departments made it possible for its students to go into sophomore or junior courses at the finest colleges in the South. For the first five years, the school was for both men and women and called Gaston College. Later it changed its name. In fact, Bess Puett was able to go straight from Gaston Female College in 1902 into medical school in Baltimore. Other students who graduated from this school included lawyers, teachers and doctors. Some of the most notable were O.F. Mason, Dr. George Holland, Claude and Lucius Holland, Dr. Carl Wolfe and A.L. Bulwinkle (U.S. congressman).

Old Gaston College, on the 200 block of South College Street, was considered a "gem of architecture." *Courtesy of the Thornburg family.*

The school had the support of the community, with many benefactors, including Jonas Hoffman Jr., M.L. Little, Henry Setzer, A.P. Rhyne, L.L. Suggs, Moses Rhyne, John Rhodes, John Rhyne, M.A. Rhyne, W.A. Mauney, J.S. Mauney, David Mauney and Ambrose Costner.[81] Some of these men were active in promoting Dallas Mill, incorporated in 1891, and other textile mills in the county. Gaston College was first a two-story building thirty by fifty feet, but later a three-story brick building one hundred feet long by forty feet wide was added and the two buildings were connected by a porch. It was a boarding school, with board and tuition ten and twelve dollars per month.

S.A. Wolfe, the music professor, traveled to Charleston to persuade Miss Hermene Bulwinkle to move to Dallas to teach Spanish and art. She later became his wife. In 1891, her family—including her sisters, Mable and Muriel, and her little eight-year-old brother, Alfred Lewis "Lee"—liked Dallas so much, they moved there with her. The Bulwinkles were teachers in the Dallas School system. Lee said that he was teaching so that he could make enough money to go to law school. Carrie Puett Lewis told of a game she and her friends made up and named in honor of two of their teachers. It was called Bulla-Wolfa—Bulla for Bulwinkle and Wolfa for Wolfe.

Teacher Institutes

In 1890, Dallas was the largest town in Gaston County, twice the size of Gastonia, with a population of 410.[82] Every fall, the state held teacher institutes in each county. The ones for Gaston County were at the courthouse, with some classes at the college. Teachers boarded at the White House Hotel, a well-known Gaston County hostelry just across the street. Several weeks of required intensive teacher training were followed by testing with pay based on the grades achieved. The teachers with the highest grades were paid thirty dollars a month. The superintendent of schools (1886–1901) was L.M. Hoffman, who wrote *Our Kin* and lived at 208 North Hoffman Street in Dallas. He planned the teacher institutes for the county and wrote, "Gaston College, located in Dallas, contributed greatly to the educational life of the entire county." A good education has always been a major goal of the people of Dallas.[83]

Tragically, in 1891, Professor Little was in a fatal train accident on his way to Hickory to help organize Lenoir-Rhyne University (then Lenoir College). He was considered the top candidate to be Lenoir-Rhyne's first president.[84]

Without Little and with the competition from state-supported public colleges and public high schools, Gaston Female College slowly declined and closed in 1905. The last commencement of old Gaston College was an impressive event held on June 9, 1905, with a reception at the White House Hotel. Miss Essie Wilson and Miss Corinne Puett were the last two graduates. There was dancing and fine food, and beautiful flowers decorated all the rooms.

For a number of years, the old college building was used as a public grade school and high school, with the Farm and Life School at the courthouse, and having an enrollment of three hundred.[85] My parents attended these schools. After the new Dallas Elementary and High School was built in 1920 on West Church Street, the college building was used as apartments for textile millworkers.[86]

Dallas School 1914 basketball players standing beside the old Gaston Female College building. The one in the middle is Winnie Thornburg. The others are unknown. *Courtesy of the Thornburg family.*

Costner and Lohr General Store

Costner and Lohr bought the old college buildings for use as a big general merchandise store. They had a successful business for twenty-five years in High Shoals. The old college buildings were in an excellent location with an acre of land on the CN&W railroad, and they had a merry-go-round in the grove. The store carried groceries, shoes, clothing, notions, hardware, caskets and furniture. It was said to have had the finest patronage of any store in Gaston County. It also had the Dallas Moving Picture Theater, the first picture show in Dallas. Burt Cloninger wrote that old-timey coffins were custom made in the shape of the person being buried with the body, head and shoulders cut out and then just a little straight box. A hole was cut in the ground the shape of the box.[87] Costner and Lohr took in $1,200 a day.[88]

On May 31, 1926, early on a Sunday morning, they had the worst fire the county had ever seen. The building burned to the ground, and the owners lost

Old-Fashioned Fruit Roll

This makes a welcomed treat in a lunch box.

1 stick butter
¾ cup flour
2 teaspoon baking powder
1 teaspoon salt
¾ cup sugar
¾ cup milk
2 cups sliced apples
Sugar to sweeten apples (berries, cherries or peaches may be used instead), about ¾ cup sugar to 1 quart raw apples.

Melt butter in pan. Make a batter by combining the flour, baking powder, salt, sugar and milk. Pour this over butter, but do not stir. Mix sliced apples with sugar and pour over batter; still do not stir. Place in 400-degree oven and bake 40 minutes. Batter rises up through apples.

Recipe from Mrs. Fred Robinson.

everything. Not even the pumps from the Dorothy and Monarch Mills, which were nearby, were enough. They were said to have had only $10,000 in insurance.

Dallas Elementary School and Dallas High School

300 BLOCK, WEST CHURCH STREET

The Dallas Elementary School, which was at first both an elementary and high school with an auditorium on the first floor, was built in 1920 on West Church Street, originally named Clay Street. My mother was in the first class to graduate in this school (in 1921), the same place where she later taught third grade. In 1922, the boys' basketball team won the area championship. The school building no longer exists. Cloninger Park now occupies that space.[89] Across the street, the 1925 Dallas High School (NRHP) holds memories for many in Dallas. Now, it is an apartment building.

Dallas School became Dallas High School and Elementary School in 1920. Its first championship basketball season was 1922.The team members were (first row, left to right) Has Clemmer, Clyde Thornburg, Brady Ratchford, (second row) Herman Thornburg, Jack Pasour, J.B. Henson (coach and principal), (third row) Claude Pasour, Beeler Lineberger and Carl Lee Hoffman. *Courtesy of Peggy Cearley.*

Wilma's Steamed Quail

Place 6 quail and 1 pound of pork in a saucepan, season with salt and pepper, cover with water and cook until tender. Remove birds, roll them in flour and brown them in butter and shortening in a frying pan. Pour broth over them and steam until gravy is thick. Take birds out of gravy before serving.

Recipe from Wilma Thornburg.

Thelma's Hot Rolls

Thelma Cloninger's rolls, the ones she made in the cafeteria at Dallas High School, will be remembered as a Dallas treasure. No other school in the county could claim better lunches for its students than Dallas. Joann Cloninger Brooks, her daughter, provided this recipe.

1 package dry yeast
2 cups lukewarm water (100 to 110 degrees)
2 quarts plain flour
13 level teaspoons sugar
2 teaspoons baking powder
½ teaspoon salt
½ cup shortening
About 1 stick margarine, more or less as needed

Better if made the day before and placed in refrigerator. Sprinkle yeast into water and let stand for a few minutes. Stir until dissolved. Sift dry ingredients into large bowl. Cut in shortening and add yeast and mix well. Refrigerate until ready to use.

To bake, take the amount of dough out of refrigerator that you want to use and roll out. Cut rolls the size you prefer. Melt margarine in pan that you are going to put the rolls in and dip rolls on both sides. Let rise two or three hours. Bake at 450 degrees and serve while still hot. Check at the grocery store in buying your yeast and be sure it is dated far ahead of the present date.

Recipe from Thelma Cloninger.

Dallas High School, built in 1925, is listed on the National Register of Historic Places. *Photo by author.*

The award-winning Dallas marching band with director Donald Deal participated in many parades. If you could see their faces, you might recognize Linda Summey, Peggy Hoffman, Wayne Ann Clemmer, Patsy Cearley, Bobby Pasour, Ray Hoyle, Gene Hoyle, Amy Puett, Fern Rhyne, Carl White Hoffman, Gene Pasour, Judy Summey, David Hoyle, Alice Kincaid, Steve Williams, Barry Clemmer, Ann Walker, Gayle Walker, Evon Houser, Clarence Thornburg Jr., Dwight Beechum, Brenda Herman, Kitty Kay Thornburg and others. *Courtesy of Peggy Cearley.*

Many remember Donald Deal, listed in the North Carolina Hall of Fame for Band Directors, and all of the drills, parades and halftimes in the 1950s. The band marched in the Charlotte Thanksgiving Parade every year and won many regional and state awards. The students in that band were very talented as well, with names you might recognize. Many took their music with them to school, college, church and wherever they went. Gene Pasour later played with Arthur Smith and the Crackerjacks and Barry Clemmer with the military band.

Many outstanding teachers taught at and notable students graduated from these schools. Two of the most well-known graduates were Dr. William C. Friday, president of the University of North Carolina from 1956 to 1986, and North Carolina state senator David Hoyle, a member of the legislature from 1993 to 2010. When Dr. Friday was asked to name one of his most influential teachers, he named Wilma Thornburg, a seventh grade teacher at Dallas. *Uncle Tom's Cabin* was one of her book selections that she always discussed with her classes long before *Brown v. the Board of Education* in 1954. Her lessons are still evident today in her students' lives, and they were evident in Bill Friday's life. She taught many lawyers, judges, scientists, ministers, business owners, professors, doctors, teachers and even a college president who had to stand strong and do the right thing during the 1960s and 1970s.

Homes in the Neighborhood

Walk the streets of Dallas, and you will see many homes of interest. The ones pictured here are on West Trade Street and West Main Street. Most homes are private residences and are not open to the general public, but they can be enjoyed from the street.

Oscar Mason Sr. Home

101 Maple Street

This home is on the corner of Maple Street and West Main Street and was built in the early 1900s. Oscar Mason was a well-known attorney in Dallas. He was the lawyer for Caroline Shipp, the last woman hanged in North Carolina, and he was successful in getting her execution delayed but not in getting the sentence lessened. Sentiment was strong against her.

This home was built for Oscar Mason, a prominent lawyer in Dallas and Gastonia. *Photo by author.*

The appeal went to the governor and was denied.[90] During the early 1900s, Oscar Mason served for ten years in the North Carolina legislature, taking over his father's senate seat. When the courthouse was moved to Gastonia in 1911, the Mason family also moved. Colonel Lawson A. Mason was Oscar Mason's father and his 1800s home still stands at 205 Stanley Road. Lawson Mason was a Confederate soldier who returned from the war, bought the Jesse Holland home on Trade Street, lived in it for many years and later, around 1890, sold it to the Dallas Mill. Colonel Mason then built his new house on the Dallas-Stanley Road, near the intersection with Trade Street.

C.C. Cornwell Home
308 WEST MAIN STREET

The Gaston County clerk of court owned this home. When the courthouse was moved to Gastonia, C.C. Cornwell and his family remained here in Dallas and just commuted the three miles back and forth.

A Grand Cole Slaw

1 apple, cut fine
2 carrots, grated
½ small head cabbage, grated
2 stalks celery, cut fine
salt to taste
¼ cup French dressing
½ cup mayonnaise

Toss first five ingredients together. Just before serving, mix the French dressing and mayonnaise and pour over slaw.

Recipe from Mrs. C.C. Cornwell

This was the home of C.C. Cornwell, who was serving as Gaston County clerk of court when the county seat moved to Gastonia, but he stayed in Dallas. *Photo by author.*

Wilkins-Houser House

212 WEST TRADE STREET

There was originally a small home on this site, built by Simon Peter Pasour. He married Dianna Broom in 1852, and they raised the first four of their eleven children here. Martha Pasour Jenkins was their third child. Her childhood home was described in her obituary, which told how much she loved growing up near the Square. The smaller home was incorporated into this large home for Dr. S.A. Wilkins, it is thought, by Moses Moore, a local builder. The Wilkinses lived here, and Dr. Wilkins had his office upstairs in the old bank building on the corner of Trade and Holland Streets. In the 1950s, the home was bought by the Blair Falls Houser family. The first floor became Dallas Funeral Home, and the second floor was the Houser residence. In the backyard was a large barn. At times, high school classes used the barn to build school projects and parade floats.

GINGER SNAPS

1 large cup combined butter and lard
1 cup sugar
1 cup molasses
1 teaspoon baking soda
½ cup of hot water
1 tablespoon ground ginger
1 tablespoon ground cinnamon
1 teaspoon ground cloves
Enough flour for pretty stiff dough

Blend the butter and lard. Combine the sugar and molasses with the butter mixture. Meanwhile, dissolve baking soda in the hot water. Then, add to sugar and butter mixture and mix. In a separate bowl, mix the spices and two cups of flour and add half of the flour mixture to the wet ingredients. Mix well and add the rest of the flour mixture. You will need to add more flour if the dough isn't stiff enough to roll out thin. If it is sticky, just add a little more flour. Roll dough thin and cut with a cookie cutter. Bake at 425 degrees, but watch them so they don't burn. These will keep for weeks. Put in tin box.

ORANGE FRUIT CAKE

This was a favorite Christmas cake.

½ cup butter
1 cup sugar
1 orange, rind grated (1 tablespoon for cake)
2 eggs
1 teaspoon baking soda
Pinch salt
2 cups flour
⅔ cup buttermilk
1 cup dates
½ cup chopped nuts

Cream butter and sugar; add 1 tablespoon of the grated orange peel. Then add eggs, one at a time. Mix together baking soda, salt and flour and add to wet ingredients. Add buttermilk and mix. Fold in dates and nuts. Bake in biscuit pan at 350 degrees. (A biscuit pan is just a square pan with two-inch sides.)

TOPPING FOR ORANGE CAKE

1 cup granulated sugar
Remainder of grated orange peel
½ cup orange juice

In a saucepan, stir together all ingredients and heat to dissolve sugar. Put on cake slowly as soon as it comes from the oven. Cut in squares.

Recipes from Mabel Craig Wilkins.

Dr. Wilkins and his family lived in this home. His office was in the old bank building. *Photo by author.*

George Detter House

216 WEST TRADE STREET

This richly detailed home was built around 1892 by master carpenter George Detter for his own family. His wife was Florence Pasour, one of Eli Pasour's ten children. The roof is the tin-tile roof known as the "Dallas Shingle" that is seen on some of the century-old homes found on Gaston, Trade and Holland Streets and was made at the tin factory on North College Street. These tiles are Dallas originals and evidently have lasted for over a century. This beautiful home is a corner landmark of Dallas with carved mantels and other interior woodwork detail. The home is surrounded by a wrought-iron fence. It is on the study list for local designation for Historic Preservation.

Eve's Apple Pie

FOR SYRUP:

1½ cups brown sugar
2 cups water

FOR DOUGH:

1 tablespoon shortening
2 tablespoon sugar
1 egg
2 cups flour
4 teaspoons baking powder
½ teaspoon salt
½ cup sweet milk
4 apples, finely chopped
Pinch cinnamon

For syrup: Combine brown sugar and water in a medium saucepan. Place on stove to boil while making dough. Boil sugar and water until sugar dissolves, stirring often.

For dough: Cream shortening and sugar and add egg. Sift together flour, baking powder and salt. Add flour alternately with milk into sugar mixture, mixing well.

Roll dough about ¼-inch thick and spread with finely chopped apples. Roll dough up, as you would a jellyroll, and cut in 1-inch pieces. Pour syrup in a baking dish and place pie roll slices on top. Dot with butter. Sprinkle with cinnamon. Bake until brown. It is delicious.

Recipe from Jonnie Detter.

George Detter and his wife, Florence Pasour Detter, lived in this home, which he built around 1892. *Photo by author.*

Grady Friday Home
217 West Trade Street

The corner where the Grady Friday family lived was once known as "Costner Corner," at the intersection of Trade and Oakland Streets and across the street from the Detter home. This corner was the site of Rufus Costner's blacksmith shop (and later Simon Peter Pasour's blacksmith shop). Rufus, son of Valentine Costner, married Herselia Pasour, daughter of Eli Pasour. This home was the home of Grady Friday, postmaster from 1936 to 1952, and Faye Sapoch Friday, the Latin teacher at the high school. In 1938, Grady Friday won the North Carolina postal trophy for submitting the most original cachet design for Hoff National Air Mail Week. The design was a picture of the Dallas Courthouse drawn by Madge White Houser. Mary Ann Friday Carpenter, the Fridays' daughter, said that the postmaster general came to Dallas to present the award.

FAYE FRIDAY'S FRUIT SALAD

2 cups marshmallows
1 can white cherries (#3-size can)
1 can shredded pineapple
½ pound almonds
Juice of 1 lemon

DRESSING:
2 eggs
1 cup milk
Salt
Pinch mustard
1 cup whipped cream

Mix first five ingredients together in a large mixing bowl. In a double boiler, combine remaining ingredients, except whipped cream. Cook until thick. Cool and then fold in whipped cream. Pour over fruit and nut mixture and refrigerate for 12 hours.

This home stands on the corner of West Trade Street and Oakland, once known as Costner Corner. *Photo by author.*

John C. Puett House
308 West Trade Street

This beautiful old home, built in 1880, was the prominent Puett family's home. It was added on to as the family grew. George Detter did much of the work on this house. It is one of the Dallas houses on the study list for local designation for historical preservation. John Collins Puett was a merchant, a mayor of Dallas and a state senator in 1917. He was the son of Reverend J.W. Puett. Dr. Bessie Violet Puett, the Puetts' second daughter, graduated from Gaston Female College in Dallas and then went to the Women's Medical College in Baltimore, Maryland. In 1909, she took her North Carolina state boards and returned to Philadelphia to do her internship at Women's Hospital. She came home to Dallas as the first female doctor in Gaston County. Dr. Bess, as she was called, made rounds at the County Home and assisted Dr. L.N. Glenn.[91] She married Reverend D.L. Jones, a Presbyterian minister. John and Mary Elizabeth Froneberger Puetts' oldest daughter was Carrie Puett Lewis, who wrote of her mother's trip to visit relatives in Texas. She brought back crape myrtles for their home, and many of the ones found

This was the home of John C. Puett and his wife, Mary Elizabeth Froneberger Puett. *Photo by author.*

in Dallas came from those trees. The crape myrtle is Dallas's official tree. In the 1960s, an effort was made to plant more of the trees around town. A younger daughter was Miss Corrine Puett, who taught piano in Dallas. She was one of the last people to graduate from the Gaston Female College. I took lessons from her and interviewed her for a report on Dallas. She allowed me to take an old, very delicate dress to school for my report. It was the dress she wore when she graduated from Gaston Female College.

Salted Pecans

Shell pecans. Place in pan and put in oven. Watch closely until light brown. Stir small amount of butter into nuts while hot. Turn onto heavy brown paper; salt to taste.

Recipe from Corinne Puett.

Uncooked Peach Pickles

2 quarts whole peeled peaches
1 large teacup vinegar*
3 large teacups sugar
Tie 1 tablespoon cloves
1 stick cinnamon in gauze

Put peeled, raw peaches in a stone crock. Bring vinegar, sugar and spices to a boil. Pour this mixture, hot, over the peaches. Weight peaches down with a saucer; cover and let stand overnight. Each morning for seven days, drain syrup from peaches, bring to a boil and then pour back over peaches. On the eighth day, thicken the syrup with a little more sugar, as the water from peaches will thin, and you will have a surplus of syrup to boil down and put back over peaches. Drop peaches into the hot syrup just long enough to heat. Pack into jars, cover and seal.

**(1 teacup equals about ¾ cup)*

Recipe from Mary Elizabeth Froneberger Puett. Printed in the 1947 Dallas Woman's Club cookbook, where this recipe was listed as being over one hundred years old.

Pinkney Summey House

Built around 1903, this Queen Anne home shows much detail.

Dallas is known not only for its beautiful homes but also for the many flowering trees and yards that surround them. The Pinkney Summey House has many flowering trees in its side yard, and Christine Clemmer's beautiful garden on Oakland Street is an example of the lovely backyard gardens found in Dallas. Dallas also has town gardens, church prayer gardens and the master gardeners' teaching garden in Dallas Park.

This Queen Anne–style home was built in 1903 for Pinkney Summey. *Photo by author.*

7
OUT IN DALLAS TOWNSHIP

When Gaston County was first carved from Lincoln County, five townships were designated. Dallas Township, as shown on a 1930 county map, included the area between the Lincoln County line to the north and Big Long Creek to the south, Pasour Mountain to the west and Spencer Mountain to the east, with the line running just west of the town of Stanley. The town of Dallas is located in the center of the county, as planned.

Dallas Park

Dallas-Cherryville Highway 279

This wonderful park has something for everyone. It also has a long history. One of the early German pioneers of this area was Sebastian Best, who married Katrina Hoyle, one of the daughters of Peter Hoyle. Their daughter Sallie married Peter Hovis, and together they had one son. After her husband and her son were gone, Sallie was alone. When Sallie Best Hovis died, she left land to two nephews, a farm to a woman who had been her lifelong slave and the rest of her land she gave to Gaston County on the condition that it be used to help the poor.[92]

Dallas Park is located on land given to Gaston County by Sallie Best Hovis to be used to help the poor. *Photo by author.*

The Gaston County Home

The Gaston County Home built in 1904 for the less fortunate was the result of her generous gift. The director and his family lived upstairs. Residents had rooms downstairs, and doctors made regular house calls. Dr. Bess was one of the doctors who tended these patients.

If she were here, Mrs. Hovis would see, standing on her old land, the County Extension Service and Community Resource Center that offer master gardener classes, canning classes, cooking with seasonal foods classes, farmers' markets, help for farmers and landowners and the senior citizen center that provides programs and activities. All year long, there are concerts, ball games, fishing, meeting places for groups in Biggerstaff Park and special events. Among the events are the Symphony Orchestra concerts in June, the Gem Show during the first week of October and the Hamfest, one of the oldest and largest gatherings of ham radio operators in the South; however,

The County Home was built in 1904 to fulfill Mrs. Hovis's wishes. *Photo by author.*

the highlight is the Cotton Ginning Days Festival, which attracts over thirty thousand visitors each second week in October with a parade, food, games, exhibits and crafts. A working cotton gin separating the seeds from the cotton fibers is the centerpiece of this festival and what the people come to see. The Cotton Ginning Days Festival is sponsored by Gaston Agriculture, Mechanical and Textile Restoration Association (GAMTRA). The earliest recorded cotton gin in this area was mentioned in John Hoffman's will, dated July 16, 1805, and was left to his son, John. It was located on the north side of the South Fork of the Catawba River.

Heritage Village

The 1890 Heritage Village at Dallas Park includes a farm, home, church and small village with blacksmith shop. The James Hillhouse White barn built in 1850 is part of the exhibit. Other buildings have been moved here. During the middle of December, these buildings become a Christmas Village with

This 1850 barn was the first building moved to Dallas Park for the early farm exhibit. *Photo by author.*

interactive handcrafted projects, festivities and hot chocolate, hot cider and cookies for anyone who would like to participate.

THE SIMON PETER PASOUR HOUSE

Dallas-Cherryville Highway 279

This house, sometimes called the Stowe-Best Home, was built in the mid-nineteenth century and is located across from the old County Home and Dallas Park. After the war, the house was bought by Simon Peter Pasour (1828–1909), great-grandson of pioneers Jacob Rhyne, Garret Wills, Jacob Hoyle and George Pasour, and the home is still owned by their descendants. It has its old details and the same structure on the same cut stone foundation as when first built. The yard with old boxwoods—planted long ago by Dianna Pasour and some of her children—was known as one of the most

Edna White's Seedless Blackberry Jam

For each quart of berries, add ¾ cups of water. Wash berries. Then mash and boil them until soft and mushy. Put pulp through a sieve and measure. For each cup of pulp, add 1 cup of sugar. Boil rapidly for 20 minutes. Put in jars. Let stand until cold. Cover with paraffin.

Originally called the Stowe-Best home, Simon Peter Pasour bought this house after the Civil War. *Photo by author.*

beautiful yards in the area. This was the childhood home where one of my grandmothers grew up. She was Edna Mae Pasour White, youngest of Simon Peter Pasour and Dianna Broom Pasour's eleven children. Simon Peter and four brothers served in the War Between the States. One, Ephriam, lost his life in the fight. Simon Peter was captured at Petersburg, Virginia, and held in prison at Fort Delaware until after the end of the war.[93]

While living at this home, my grandmother was witness to one of the most tragic events described earlier, the last hanging in Gaston County, which took place on the cold day of January 22, 1892, near the old County Home. Caroline Shipp, a condemned African American woman convicted of killing her child, came riding in a wagon. She sat on top of her casket, staring around at the crowd of people who came to watch, and leaned down to speak to some she knew, telling them that she did not kill her baby. As she rode up to the hanging tree, she sang softly, "Why do we mourn departing friends/Or shake at death's alarms/'Tis but the voice that Jesus sends/To call them to his arms," an Isaac Watts hymn. My grandmother said Caroline was the calmest person there. Caroline told the crowd that she wasn't afraid because she would be with her baby again soon.[94]

Simon Peter Pasour was a blacksmith and a furniture builder. He had a shop near his home and one on "Costner Corner" and was said to be an expert at making grain cradles and farm tools. Edna Mae was very talented, also. Her father taught her to make furniture, and her mother taught her to quilt. She made quilts, which now are treasured heirlooms in all of those families, for all twelve of her grandchildren.

James Hillhouse White House

White and Jenkins Road

James Hillhouse White was born in Derry, Ireland, in 1802 and came to the United States in 1818 with his mother and brother. His father was a weaver who had traveled from castle to castle in Ireland weaving for families. In the United States, he traveled between Charleston and New York selling his woolen broadcloth, some of which is still in the family. He came over before the rest of the family to set up a homestead and earn enough money for his wife's and sons' passages. The homestead the father set up was on Big Long Creek near Bradley Creek, and there, the two boys, James and Barry White, lived with their parents. The parents' homestead was located between where the Dallas-Gastonia Highway (becomes Gaston Street in Dallas) and Highway 321 are now, near the Rankin Lake Road. (Standing chimneys from the old homestead were still visible from Highway 321 in the 1950s.)

James was sixteen years old in 1818 when he arrived in North Carolina. As a young man, James worked at Henry Fulenwider's pig iron forge on Big Long Creek at Pasour Mountain and became one of his favorites. Jacob Fulenwider

James Hillhouse White lived here when he served in the general assembly during the formation of Gaston County. *Photo by author.*

had built a tramway that ran the six miles between the old forge on Long Creek and his furnace and ironworks at High Shoals on the South Fork. The tramway was located near where Puetts' Chapel Church Road is now and had wood rails with wagons drawn by mules and ran near the base of the mountain. By watching the tramway, James saw firsthand the value of a railroad. Henry Fulenwider took the young James White under his wing and educated him.

In 1834, James met and married Margaret "Peggy" Jenkins, daughter of David and Nancy Carpenter Jenkins, and became interested in public affairs. James and Peggy settled near the White and Jenkins Mill and Shoals and built their home. James Hillhouse White was elected to the house of commons from Lincoln County in 1842, 1844 and 1846, and he spearheaded the formation of Gaston County and served on the committee to divide Lincoln County into two separate counties. (Barry White died in his brother's home following wounds from the Mexican War.)

When Gustavus Miller, a representative from Davie County, introduced the bill for Gaston County, it did not have enough support to pass. James Hillhouse White tabled the bill and later brought it back when it had the support needed.[95] (Robert Carpenter said that "White was a very significant leader in Gaston County and it was through his efforts that Gaston County was created in 1846.") White was reelected in 1848 and again in 1850 as the state senator from Lincoln and Gaston Counties, making him Gaston County's first elected state senator. In 1854, 1860 and 1862, he was elected from Gaston County, serving in the legislature for sixteen years. In May 1861, after President Lincoln called for seventy-five thousand troops to invade the South, White signed the Ordinance of Secession and sent word from Raleigh to Robert Lewis in Dallas to immediately gather the supplies from White and Jenkins Mill to be used by the Gaston County troops. Six of his sons volunteered to fight in the War Between the States, two of whom were killed. (Larkin was eighteen years old when he was killed at Petersburg. David, age twenty, was killed on June 27, 1862, at Gaines Mill. Henry was wounded in May 1862 at Seven Pines.)[96]

James Hillhouse White's oldest son, Thaddeus, survived the war and was my great-grandfather. (Thaddeus married Eliza Costner, daughter of Valentine Costner, and great-great-granddaughter of Adam Costner.) Senator White considered the securing of the charters for railroads his greatest service to the county. During Reconstruction, buildings were burned, including the home of Reverend Peterson, who was the Dallas Lutheran minister. James Hillhouse and Peggy Jenkins White are buried in the White and Jenkins Cemetery with many of their family and other kin. The original home of James Hillhouse White and Peggy Jenkins White burned in a fire in 1885 and was rebuilt the same year it burned by his son Samuel Jasper White on the same stone foundation from the original 1834 house. In a speech given almost a century later, Dr. William C. Friday quoted Senator White, as he voted in the election of 1880, as saying, "I was born in a land of tyranny but want to die in a land of liberty."

Sidney Shields White Home

On the White Farm

The fifth child of Simon Peter Pasour was Henrietta "Etta" Pasour. She married Sidney Shields White, a son of James Hillhouse White. This was their

Sidney Shields and Etta Pasour White had a home on the White farm near the White and Jenkins Cemetery. *Photo by author*

home. Sidney Shields was a Confederate soldier.[97] Later, the house became the home of one of their sons, Augustus "Gus" White. It sits on part of the old White and Jenkins farm and was built in 1884. The 100th anniversary of Gaston County was celebrated in October 1946, and chronicles of the time record: "Among the officials who staged the celebration and were in the audience were descendants of the Whites, the Hollands, the Rankins, the Rhynes, the McLeans, Loves, Wilsons, Plonks, Mauneys, Johnstons, and others who had founded Gaston County a century before."[98]

L.A. Thornburg Home

Thornburg Road

The home of Larkin Andrew and Sarah Cloninger Thornburg was built in 1893. They were my great-grandparents. My dad was born here. (It was the

Larkin Andrew and Sarah Cloninger Thornburg's home was built in 1893. *Photo by author.*

D.S. Thornburg home, my grandparents' home, when I was young, and I was here three or four times a week and again on Sunday afternoons.) The home where Larkin grew up was a log cabin on this farm, but built farther back, and it no longer stands. Many people in North Carolina did not believe in slavery; many Thornburgs were among them. Later, L.A. Thornburg was to write about the year he was fourteen years old, the year before the War Between the States: "At the outbreak of the Civil War, feeling naturally ran high. The Federal Union, Secession, War—these were the leading topics for conversation at all gatherings and wherever friends met, in the home or in the public places. Everything was overshadowed by the clouds of war. In those gloomy days, I had many opportunities of hearing my father discuss these important questions with my uncle who lived near my home. They were not in favour of the war."[99] The state voted against leaving the Union. It wasn't until it became clear that the North planned to invade the South that North Carolina went into the war. It paid dearly, losing more soldiers than any other state in the bloodiest war our country has known. The Civil War wasn't forgotten, but most people tried to put it behind them. Larkin was fourteen when the war began. The year he turned seventeen, he fought in the Battle of Cedar Creek on October 18 and 19, 1864. This battle was one of the last attempts of the South to invade the North and take Washington. There is a lot of controversy about that battle because there are several hours of unaccounted time. Larkin believed the Civil War was a "rich man's war; a poor man's fight." He returned home and served

How to Make Sausage

5-pound Boston butt pork roast or shoulder, ⅓ fat, ⅔ lean
1½ tablespoon salt
1 tablespoon black pepper
1 tablespoon sage

Cut meat, season with salt and pepper and grind it with the sage. Make a patty, cook and taste it. Adjust seasoning to your taste. You may wish to add a few drops of hot sauce. (The key is to "adjust the seasoning to your own taste.")

Recipe from Clarence O. Thornburg

his county by being on the board of education for many years. The county commissioners and the board of education were considered the county's two strongest appointed governing groups.

On Little Long Creek at Thornburg Shoals is where L.A. Thornburg's family had a sawmill. His son, D.S. Thornburg, had a dairy and sold his milk to a new business in Gastonia, Tony's Ice Cream Company. C.O. Thornburg drove the wagon to deliver the milk. The children of Ellen Pasour Thornburg, after they grew up and had homes of their own, would make sausage, taste it and take it to her to taste and wait for her to declare, "Oh, that's good—best ever."

Antioch Lutheran Church

Costner Community

This is the "old" church building built in 1883, and in the background is the "new" church, almost across the road from Costner School. During the August 31, 1886 earthquake in Charleston, a wall in this building was cracked. The wall of the old Presbyterian Church in Dallas on the corner of Church and College Streets cracked at the same time. Many Pasour family

MRS. PASOUR'S HOMEMADE LIGHT BREAD

1 cup scalded milk
2 tablespoons salt
4 tablespoons sugar
1 package yeast dissolved in 1 cup lukewarm (100 to 110 degrees) water
5 tablespoons lard, melted
2 cups (or more) flour

Cool milk to lukewarm and stir in salt and sugar. Stir in the yeast water. Add lard and flour and make the dough. Add enough flour to keep dough from being sticky. Start with 2 cups flour and add more as you need it. Put it in a warm place to rise, about 1½ hours. Take out, work out air bubbles and place in greased pans. Let rise another 1½ hours and bake.

Recipe from Hazel Marie Carpenter Pasour.

Antioch Lutheran Church was built in 1883. Both the Pasour and the Ratchford family reunions are held here. *Photo by author.*

reunions and picnics have been held here. The Ratchford reunions are also held here at Antioch. Parents told impatient little ones to "get a [country] ham biscuit and stand and wait" for the grown-ups to be served first. Many members of early pioneer families are buried in this cemetery.

St. Paul's Lutheran Church

Hardin Community

An earlier building was destroyed by fire on May 27, 1987 during a severe thunderstorm, and this one was built to be almost like the old one.

A story told by Lillian Senter Kinney, whose father was the minister at St. Paul's in the late 1800s and early 1900s, explains her schooling in the home of a neighbor, Dave Friday, grandfather of William C. Friday. Mr. Dave did not consider four months of public instruction enough for his children, so he hired a live-in teacher to continue classes, and he invited the Senters' children to join in the home schooling. He felt a good education should be available to those willing to study for it. Later, Lillian attended high school at old Gaston College, boarding during the week and going home on weekends. She said she loved getting up early on Monday morning and watching the sun come up as she and her father drove past Spencer Mountain in the family buggy. Hardin School

The St. Paul's Lutheran Church building was destroyed by fire and rebuilt in the 1980s. *Photo by author.*

was built almost across the road from St. Paul's Lutheran Church in 1924 on land donated by Emily Friday. The Costners and the Thornburgs have family reunions at St. Paul's.

COLONEL W.G. MORRIS HOUSE

Ratchford Drive and Cloninger Road

This home was built in 1878 on the site of an earlier, smaller house that was moved back to be the kitchen. It was the home of Colonel William Groves Morris (1825–1918) and his wife, Louisa Costner. He helped build many of the older homes, barns and bridges in this community, as well as the gold and iron mills at High Shoals and the branch mint in Charlotte. He was the second-highest-ranking soldier in Gaston County in the Civil War, Company H, North Carolina Thirty-seventh Regiment, and survived twenty battles before being captured at Gettysburg during Pickett's Charge. At Gettysburg, one in every four Confederate soldiers killed was from North Carolina, mainly because of Pickett's Charge. One North Carolina Regiment, the Twenty-sixth, went into the Battle of Gettysburg with eight hundred soldiers, and three days later only eighty had survived.[100] Between one-fifth and one-fourth of the entire Confederate army was from North Carolina.[101] Lee had ordered Pickett to take Cemetery Ridge with fifteen thousand men. Ten Gaston County men were killed and twenty-three were wounded in that one charge. They were greatly outnumbered. Morris was captured, but he broke his sword between logs of a stable so Union soldiers would not get it. He was on Johnson's Island in Lake Erie in prison for eighteen months. Stories of bravery surround his name.[102]

During the Battle of Chancellorsville in 1863, Morris's men were lying by a railroad using the rails to steady their aim. He was standing in order to see the enemy. His men begged him to lie down, but he refused. When his foot was shot, he told his men if he had been lying down, it would have been his head.[103] Out of prison and back in Gaston, he served one term in the state legislature in 1876–77, and he farmed his land.

I know this house because one of my mother's twin sisters, Leola White, married Samuel Morris Wilson, grandson of Colonel Morris, so it was also the home of my aunt and uncle. My family can remember one very hard winter in the 1940s when the snow was so deep that the Wilson family visited ours in a horse-drawn sleigh.

Idaho Baked Potato Soup

1 pound Idaho potatoes
1 quart chicken soup from stock or canned chicken broth
(or hot milk, do not boil)
½ cup cream
1 tablespoon minced parsley
Pinch paprika

First, bake the potatoes until the skins are crisp and the insides mealy. No cold baked potato can be used. Prepare a quart of well-seasoned chicken soup from stock or canned chicken broth. If you do not have chicken broth, hot milk is good. Put your freshly baked potatoes through a sieve into the hot broth. Add cream. Put minced parsley in the bottom of a soup tureen, and pour the soup mixture over it. Add a sprinkle of paprika on top.

Recipe from Leola White Wilson.

Colonel William Groves Morris and Louisa Costner Morris lived in this house built on land given to them by her father. The kitchen was an earlier construction. *Photo by author.*

DAVID RUFUS PASOUR HOME

Carr Road

David Rufus Pasour (1838–1921) was the son of David Pasour and Hannah Rhyne and the brother of Simon Peter Pasour. David Rufus and Lavinia Withers Pasour were my great-grandparents. My grandmother, one of the daughters of David Rufus, was Martha Ellen Pasour, and she married D.S. Thornburg, son of L.A. Thornburg. David Rufus fought under Stonewall Jackson and during the Battle of Cedar Run (Company A, Twenty-eighth North Carolina Regiment); he was wounded and left for dead. He lay on the battlefield for three days. The worms had gotten into his wounded arm, but it is thought by the family that they saved his life because no gangrene ever developed. Following the amputation of his right arm, he was honorably discharged on February 12, 1863.[104] For many years, he worked in the Gaston County Courthouse in Dallas as the county treasurer. Some correspondence exists between family members and soldiers, and the following letter was received by David Rufus from his brother Eli Franklin Pasour, who had been wounded and was in the Jefferson Davis Soldiers Home in Gulfport, Mississippi. This letter belonged to his granddaughter, my aunt Mary Ellen Thornburg, who allowed me to have a copy:

> *Dear Brother Rufus*
> *I am in health but not well*[.] *I* [read] *your kind letter some time ago*[.] *I was sorry to hear that Charlie lost some of his horses but was a great loss*[.] *We have had some dry weather but had a nice rain last week*[.] *I have been thinking about writing to Col Morris for some information as to the place at Gettysburg where he was wounded the 3rd of July*[.] *I have heard it was at a small house near the Yankee lines*[.] *Col Garden was also wounded at or near the Yankee lines*[.] *He was Col—34th NC*[.] *I helped him off of the field for which he thanks me very much*[.] *He told me he was a British Subject and did not want the Damn Yankees to get a hold of him*[.] *Our flag officer was killed about the same time Capt Evans saved the flag from being captured so no more from your humble Brother Eli. Excuse this badly written letter for I am very nervous this morning*[.]

After his wife, Lavinia, died, David Rufus married Minnie Maxwell, and their daughter, Ruth, was born in 1916. Her oldest half-sister was fifty years old when she was born. Ruth remembered going with her

Grandmother's Cucumber Pickles

Wash cucumbers and put in salt water and leave overnight. Rinse next morning. Use ½ part water and ⅔ part vinegar and ½ cup sugar per quart cucumbers. Heat water, vinegar, sugar and spices. Add cucumbers and stir until heated. Put in jars and seal.

Recipe from Ellen Pasour Thornburg.

Aunt Winnie's Toasty Cheese Loaf

1 cup ground cooked ham

¼ cup pickle relish
¼ cup chopped celery
1 hard-cooked egg, chopped
3 tablespoons mayonnaise
1 unsliced sandwich loaf
2 or 3 tablespoons of butter, softened
1 can cranberry sauce, cut lengthwise in ¼-inch slices
1 container sharp cheddar spreading cheese

Combine first five ingredients to make ham salad. Set aside. Trim crusts from unsliced sandwich loaf, and cut in thirds, lengthwise. Butter the bottom slice. Top with ham salad filling and middle slice of bread. Butter the middle slice. Top with cranberry sauce and top slice of bread. Cover top slice with sharp spreading cheese; toast loaf for about two minutes. Watch carefully so it does not burn. Slice to serve.

Recipe from Winnie Thornburg, principal at Costner School, daughter of D.S. Thornburg and Ellen Pasour Thornburg and granddaughter of David Rufus Pasour.

David Rufus Pasour's family lived in this home. He fought in the Civil War under Stonewall Jackson. *Photo by author.*

parents to the "Old Soldiers' Reunion." Ruth Pasour Gryder died on November 13, 2010. She was five years old when her father died. I can remember talking with her at times when she visited my grandmother, who was one of her half-sisters.

Philadelphia Lutheran Church

Philadelphia Church Road, North of Town

According to the church's written history, Philadelphia Lutheran Church (founded in 1767) is the oldest Lutheran church west of the Catawba River and the second-oldest church in Gaston County. In part, the records note:

> *The history of the church goes back to the Southern Rhine country in Germany known as Palatinate. During the first half of the 18th century, political and religious conflict in that area brought on the ravages of war and persecution which forced many inhabitants to seek asylum in the New*

> *World. They came in anticipation of life in a land where they could cherish the Word of God, and where fruits of faith could flourish. Among the people who fled their native country were Adam Kastner (Costner), his wife and five children. They sailed from Rotterdam, Holland, by way of England, and arrived in America aboard the ship* Patience *in September, 1748. After only a short stay in York County, Adam brought his family south into Piedmont North Carolina…*
>
> *The Kastners, along with the other pioneers who came, brought with them the customs, language and religion which had been part of their lives. They had land to clear and homes to build, but they never forgot the importance of religion. Sometime before the close of 1767, a meeting was held in the home of Adam Kastner. At this time, plans were made for the establishment of a church. Services continued to be held in different homes until the church was built near the South Fork River. It is reasonably sure the first church of logs was near the old Philadelphia Church cemetery. Adam Kastner can well be called the founder of this congregation. In fact, the church bore his name until 1776.*[105]

There is no reason given as to why the name of the church was changed, but many of the members think it was because the church wanted to have a biblical name, which is the tradition in the Lutheran Church. If so, the church is named for the Church of Philadelphia from the Book of Revelations in the Bible. The old Costner Church was said to have had two front doors, one for men and one for women, and a side door for women to leave with children, if necessary.

Among the early members of Philadelphia Lutheran (then Costner) Church were Adam Costner and his wife; Peter and Jacob Costner and their wives; Andrew and Thomas Costner; Margaret Costner; Mary Costner and her husband, Phillip Rudisill (all part of Adam Costner's family); Phillip's brother Michael Rudisill; Nicholas Friday and his wife, Mary Ramseur Friday (Nicholas Friday was on the Lincoln County Safety Committee, and the county court met in his home during part of 1783–84); George Hovis and his wife, Elizabeth Best Hovis; the Lineberger brothers, Peter, Lewis and John; Catherine Hoyle; and Mary Hoyle, the wife of John Henry Whittenburg.

On July 16, 1916, the most terrible flood in the memory of the area occurred. Water rose in the Philadelphia Church to within eighteen inches of the eaves. It was decided to relocate the church to higher ground. A new cemetery was started next to the new church. It was during this same 1916 flood that water in the Catawba River rose fifty-five feet, taking out the Southern Railway Bridge and flooding large mills along its way. Nineteen workmen who were on the Southern Railway Bridge at the time trying to brace the trestle fell

Philadelphia Lutheran Church, founded in 1767, is the oldest Lutheran church in the country west of the Catawba River. *Photo by author.*

from the bridge; six were rescued. The flood also did much damage to smaller buildings on rivers and creeks, washing away sawmills and destroying homes. Much of western North Carolina and the Piedmont suffered from the flood. It is interesting to note that there was a similar flood in 1816 that took out early mills along the Catawba River in Lincoln County.

CLEMMER-SHELL HOUSE

Philadelphia Church Road

This house was built in 1840 by George Clemmer II. It is one of the oldest of the Civil War–era houses still standing in the Dallas area, just off the Philadelphia Church Road. Yankee soldiers camped in the front yard of this home at the end of the Civil War. They were also camped next door at the Dixon home and on Court Square. Yankees were there in Court Square before the first Confederate soldiers returned from the war. The Clemmer-Shell house is a two-story home with an ell (wing) added to connect the kitchen to the rest of the home, as was done with many of the old homes. The Clemmer family lived in the home for about sixty years, and then the Shell family made it their home. Their descendants still live here.

The Civil War was fought mainly on Southern soil. When the Yankee troops came through, they took whatever was wanted: meat from the smoke house, corn from the cornfield and bread off the table, leaving little for the family to eat. Near the end of the war, March to May 1865, with orders to "destroy but not battle," Union general George Stoneman's troops raided North Carolina in one of the longest raids of the war. Their raids went into Lincoln County near Cottage Home. Then, they rode into the northern part of Dallas Township, bringing more destruction as they made their way west from Salisbury.[106] There are many stories of Yankee troops camped on farms and in front yards during this same time in the northern part of Dallas Township, and there are even artifacts from the Yankee soldiers who camped there and, in this case, gave them as gifts to the Confederates. Governor Zebulon B. Vance was captured in Statesville and put in prison in Washington, D.C. Many others, it was said thousands, were taken prisoner.

Stoneman had five thousand to six thousand men under his command, spread out in a line in small groups so that their destruction could cover a wide area, in a way similar to how Sherman was going through Georgia. Stoneman's plan was to destroy everything that could be of use to the Confederates—factories, bridges, railroad lines, crops and other supplies. According to Kathy Herran in *They Married Confederate Officers*, "Stoneman was as much feared in NC as Sheridan was in VA and Sherman was in GA;"[107] however, his high respect for Stonewall Jackson was evident in a rare act. While raiding Lincoln County, he took General Jackson's horse, Little Sorrel. Anna Jackson sent one of her nephews to General Stoneman requesting the return of her husband's horse. The nephew came back with the horse and a note of apology. General Jackson died following the Battle of Chancellorsville (May 1863). Seventeen years earlier, Jackson had been one of the officers in the 1846 graduating class at West Point Military Academy, and so was his roommate, George Stoneman. It was Sherman at the Bennett Farmhouse near Durham who, on April 26, 1865, accepted the surrender of all North Carolina Confederate troops, seventeen days after Appomattox. In 1867, a state convention was called to rewrite North Carolina's constitution in terms that were approved in Washington. In the state constitution, resolutions were

LIVER MUSH

Cook hog liver and one half of hog's head until it will separate from bone. When meat is done, take from broth and cool until it can be handled. Take skin from meat and grind in food chopper. Return meat to broth, season with salt, pepper and sage to taste. Let broth come to a good boil. Thicken with cornmeal, about 2 quarts, mixed with 3 or 4 tablespoons of flour. Stir constantly while meat is being added to broth to keep from lumping. Add wet meal slowly, stirring frequently until meal is thoroughly done. Pour into pans. When cool, slice and fry in grease until brown.

Recipe from Tessie Shell.

The Clemmer-Shell home was built in 1840. Union soldiers camped on this land following the Civil War. *Photo by author.*

passed to establish a uniform school system and universal male suffrage, but it wasn't until the ratification of the Fifteenth Amendment that slavery was abolished in North Carolina and black men given the right to vote. It would be over fifty more years until white and black women would gain the same privilege, which they did on August 18, 1920, when the Nineteenth Amendment to the U.S. Constitution gave all women the right to vote. (The amendment giving women the right to vote was introduced once before to the North Carolina General Assembly in 1897, and it was sadly referred to the committee on insane asylums.)[108]

During Reconstruction, hardship continued, and Dallas suffered, as did most of the South.[109] Unfortunately, there were demonstrations and acts of violence involving the Ku Klux Klan and other organized groups. The Klan had come up from York, South Carolina, and started new groups in the area. Parts of the South were under military rule until 1876. Most folks tried to make do and make the best of the situation as life went on. Times were difficult. Food was scarce. Nothing was wasted. The motto was "Use everything and use it well."

The Andrew Hoyle Homestead (NRHP)

Dallas-Stanley Road

This home, located on the Andrew Hoyle track of land outside Dallas at 1214 Dallas-Stanley Highway, was built in the late 1700s (exact date unknown) and is the oldest standing home in Gaston County. It was built using corner-post construction and is considered the last home of its type still existing in North Carolina. Andrew Hoyle (1771–1857) was a son of John Hoyle and Margaret Costner Hoyle and a grandson of Peter Hoyle (1710–1781) and Katherine Dales Hoyle, pioneers of the Hoyle family who arrived in the colonies from Germany in 1738 on the ship *Robert and Alice*. The house is on the site of John Hoyle's 1764 land grant. Andrew Hoyle acquired the land in 1794. He was a farmer, a merchant and an entrepreneur. Known as "Rich Andrew," he was one of the most prosperous people in the area. He had also been in the North Carolina legislature representing Lincoln County in the early 1800s. The Tavern Hotel and the old Presbyterian Church of Dallas were built by him. The Hoylesville post office, the first federal post office in current-day Gaston County, was located on this land near the house around 1817 with Andrew Hoyle as the first postmaster, a position he kept for most

The Andrew Hoyle homestead, built in the late 1700s, is the oldest home in Gaston County. *Photo by author.*

of his life. Winchester Pegram, in Dallas, became postmaster after Andrew Hoyle's death in 1857. An old friend of Peter Hoyle's, fellow early pioneer Sebastian Best, was said to have had his home across the creek and back in the woods on the hill across from this house.

The Hoyle Historic Homestead hosts an open house at the Andrew Hoyle House in September complete with genealogical discussions and Revolutionary reenactors. Three hundred people attend this annual event, and the public is invited.

THE ELI HOYLE HOME (NRHP)

Dallas-Stanley Road

Eli Hoyle, one of Andrew's sons, built this Federal-style home in 1832 almost across the road from his father. He was a farmer and a merchant and owned

Eli Hoyle's home was built in 1832 across from Andrew Hoyle's home. *Photo by author.*

a large plantation. Andrew and Eli Hoyle bought the High Shoals Iron Works around 1840 and, along with it, the twelve thousand acres of land on which it stood. It became known as A&E Hoyle Company Iron Works. Eli died just a few years later in 1844.[110]

One of Peter Hoyle's granddaughters, Hannah, married George Pasour Jr., and they were grandparents of Simon Peter Pasour, David Rufus Pasour, Eli Pasour (the first mayor of Dallas) and forty-eight others. Many people in the area trace their ancestors to the Hoyles and the Pasours. However, by now, many pioneer families are kin to one another in some way, since they have been here so long and have so many descendants.

PART III
WHERE THE LIVING IS GOOD

8
DALLAS OF TODAY

Take One Step Back and Two Steps Forward in Dallas

Today, Dallas is a lovely place to visit and spend the afternoon. It was planned that way from the start. Take one step back with the town and its fascinating history. It gives you the opportunity to explore the many hands-on exhibits at the Gaston County Museum of Art and History and to walk around the Square. There are gathering places to greet friends and neighbors in Dallas at the Square or at one of the restaurants in town. (Dallas also has several very good fish camps and seafood places on the edge of town, two of which, Long Creek Fish Fry and North Star Seafood, have been recommended recently online [ourstate.com] by the *North Carolina* state magazine.) For two steps forward, go to Dallas Park and the college. The park offers many special events, including horse shows and festivals for the whole family. It has a beautifully expanded learning garden and places to jog around the lake, have a picnic and attend a ball game. Something is always going on. If learning something new is what you're looking for, try Gaston College's huge offering of options at its main campus in Dallas, from discovering your ancestors to completing an associate's degree or signing up for a special class to attending a Rhythm and Blues Festival with beach music. Learn a new skill. Make something beautiful. Some people still make quilts. There are others who do carving, whittling and pottery. Dallas is a great place to visit, explore and learn.

This quilt was made from headscarves worn by women during the time of World War II. Notice the war motifs. *Photo by author.*

HOW TO TRACE YOUR ANCESTORS AND DISCOVER YOUR DALLAS CONNECTIONS

Today, many families research and collect information on ancestors, and frequently this information is shared on websites and in printed form in family books. It is easy for even the best of these sources to have a few errors, so care is needed. However, if you are looking for information on many of the pioneer families of Dallas and Dallas Township, you may wish to begin with one of the following resources or other "family" books.

Our Kin, written by L.M. Hoffman in 1915, provides information on the Best, Clemmer, Cloninger, Costner, Friday, Gaston, Hambright, Hoffman, Holland, Hovis, Hoyle, Jenkins, Lineberger, Pasour, Plonk, Puett, Rhyne, Rudisill, Shetley, Thornburg, White, Wills and Withers families, as well as other early settlers. This book is a good place to start because Miles Hoffman knew most of these people. He was born in Lincoln County in 1846, in what became Gaston, and was a son of Jonas Hoffman Jr. Both father and son were Confederate soldiers—Jonas with Lee at Appomattox and Miles under Johnston at his surrender to Sherman. Miles worked for the North Carolina state treasurer and was a law partner of U.S. congressman L.C. Gause. He managed Dallas Cotton Mills, taught Latin and Greek at Gaston Female College, was a Gaston County superintendent of schools and a member of Holy Communion Lutheran Church. He lived in Dallas at 208 North Hoffman Street, and his home is still there on the corner.

Pasour, Paysour, Payseur, Paseur, Together…At Last, written by Thomas J. Marino, gives a history of the large Pasour family. The pioneer was George Pasour. Land was granted to this family by King George III of England. There are other books on other families as well. Look for your family's book at the gift shop at the museum or attend your family's reunion. A reunion has the added benefit of the excellent food offered with the opportunity to meet kin.[111]

If you are really serious, the genealogy class at Gaston College, Dallas, with Robert Carpenter, president of the Gaston-Lincoln Genealogical Society, is a great place to learn history and genealogy. He has written a number of books, including *Carpenters' A-Plenty*, and is sought out by people from across the United States. He is one of the leading experts in our area, highly respected and frequently quoted for accuracy and depth of his research. His class directs you to the best primary sources for research at the North Carolina State Archives in Raleigh. He has been honored by the state with The Order of the Long Leaf Pine.

Some Internet sites you might find useful are Censusfinder.com, Genealogybank.com, LearnNC.edu, NCleg.net, NCpedia.org and USGENArchives.com, and there is also NCGENArchives.com to search for family or to learn more about any of the subjects mentioned in this book. In addition, the Lincoln and Gaston Counties public libraries have an online index to help you find what you need.

The "new" Gaston College—a state community college with five thousand students each term and sixteen thousand annually, built in 1964 on Highway 321 and soon to be fifty years old—was named for old Gaston College on South College Street in Dallas. The two schools actually have some things in common but no official connection. Both schools gained statewide respect and enticed out-of-state students to come take classes. What was once said about the old college can be said about the new: "Gaston College located in Dallas contributes greatly to the educational life of the entire county." However, old Gaston College was unique in that it attested to the high value placed on education here in the late 1800s.

As Rita Wehunt-Black noted in her book *Gaston County North Carolina: A Brief History*, "Dallas retained and cherished [its] old buildings and

[its] history." As the first municipality in the county, it has more historic buildings than any of the other towns in Gaston County. The *Charlotte Observer* reported on November 16, 1979, that Dallas has North Carolina's second-largest grouping in the National Register of Historical Places (only Old Salem has more) and not all of the homes that could qualify have been registered. Dallas is different than re-created villages because Dallas is real. People still live their lives in these homes. In the 1983 book *Tar Heel Sights*, Dallas was described as having "an idyllic small-town atmosphere and an architecturally rich group of commercial and residential buildings centered around a Greek revival courthouse." Few towns like it remain, because, with only a few very sad exceptions, it hasn't been turned into something artificial or destroyed as so many other towns have. We hope it will always continue to be a living town where the people appreciate and live in the historic old houses and make them their homes. In some cases, descendants of the early pioneer families still own and live in these private homes. That's what makes Dallas different. This is its heritage. Dallas is a living history lesson in itself.

Pasour Reunion in 1929 was attended by families of Simon Peter Pasour's and David Rufus Pasour's children. Many of Peter Pasour's family are on the right side and Rufus Pasour's are on the left. In the center, seated on the ground, are Muriel Taylor and Lois Sisk. The ladies seated in chairs are daughters of Peter Pasour and Rufus Pasour. People who have been identified are Edna Pasour White, Martha Pasour Jenkins, Etta Pasour White, D.S. Thornburg standing in center with hat, Winnie Thornburg, Mary Ellen Thornburg, Helen Brown, Clara Edwards, Glenn Cloninger, Bill Thornburg, Edna Rhyne Robertson, Jesse Rhyne and Lola Clemmer are to the right side. Reverend Dorus Rudisill is in the back. You may know more. *Courtesy of the Thornburg family.*

9
DOWN-HOME SOUTHERN FOODS

Recipes from Dallas with Lots of Heart and History, Treasures All

Over seventy-five recipes are included in this book to help tell the story of Dallas, to enhance the sense of place and to honor the women of Dallas and the role they have played in its history. Many of these recipes are over one hundred years old. Some are family recipes; however, many are being shared with you by the Dallas Woman's Club. Dallas is well known for family reunions, church suppers, picnics and all types of get-togethers, as well as real southern food and hospitality.

Southern food has a little Native American, English and African in it with a fair amount of Scotch, Irish and German mixed in, but it shows the hard times, deprivation and "can do" determination needed to get through. There is a lot of creativity added for good measure and the need to use everything and use it well. Real southern cooking is comfort food, whatever its origin, distinctive and authentic with a lot of love. Some tend to call it "down home" cooking, and others just say "soul food"; either way, it is a way of life and a symbol of home. It is your favorite bowl of banana pudding, a dish of homemade peach ice cream, a slice of pecan pie or a beautiful, vine-ripe tomato, just picked and sliced and in your first sandwich of the season. Dallas reminds you of sitting on the screened porch with family and friends in the early evening. The flavors are all here.

LINEBERGER'S MAPLE SPRINGS FARM

Dallas-Stanley Highway

Much less than one hundred years ago, most of Dallas Township was made up of farms. People grew their food, and they hunted and trapped animals (squirrels, birds, rabbits, deer and 'possum—my grandmother's favorite) for meat. They churned their butter, cured their hams and smoked their meats. Some people still do this. David and Thelma Thornburg have their children and their grandchildren over for a canning party every summer and fall, and they put up enough vegetables for the winter for the whole family, making sure that they reserve enough of the harvest to share with neighbors and friends and anyone else who might need a little extra—just like David's parents and his grandparents did. The skills are passed down from generation to generation. This is not uncommon; most farm families do this. David and many other master gardeners, through the North Carolina Extension Service at Dallas Park, go into the county schools and teach third graders how to garden. They have classes at school twice a week and sometimes at camps during the summer. Many playgrounds and most schoolyards have a corner for gardening. If you did not grow up learning how to garden, can and make preserves, classes are given at the North Carolina Extension Service at Dallas Park and other places in the county. The Extension Service also holds pie-baking contests and invites everyone to come by, taste the pies and vote for their favorite. Today, you will find "century farms," small farms and one of the best-known markets in Gaston County, Lineberger's, right here in Dallas Township. You can always depend on beautiful produce.

Lineberger's Maple Spring Farm Market offers farm produce that you can pick yourself. *Photo by author.*

BLACKBERRY JAM CAKE

1 cup butter
2 cups white sugar
4 eggs (whites beaten separately until soft peaks form)
1 teaspoon ground cinnamon
1 teaspoon ground cloves
4½ cups sifted flour
1 cup buttermilk
1 teaspoon baking soda dissolved in buttermilk
1 cup blackberry jam (may use the recipe in this book for jam or store-bought jam)

Cream butter and sugar. Add yolks of 4 eggs, spices, then add flour and buttermilk alternately. Add jam and fold in beaten egg whites. Bake in layers in moderate (350-degree) oven and put together with plain icing.
Recipe from Corinne Puett.

My mother, Kitty White Thornburg, used to tell a story about when she was little. One day, one of her aunts (one of Edna Pasour White's sisters) came driving up in a buggy at their farm in Costner Community, and when she saw my grandmother, she said, "Now Edney, I've come to spend the day with you, and I don't want you to go to any trouble at all for me. When I turned in up at the road, I noticed a big, fat hen in the yard. You can just get it and stew it, and make some of your good old chicken 'n dumplings. And I passed that big old apple tree just full of apples. You can pick some of those, and make a couple apple pies and some biscuits, get a few vegetables out of your garden. That'll be fine. Don't go to any extra trouble for me!" (This was around 1908.)

Edna's Crumbly Top Apple Pie

¼ cup sugar
¾ teaspoon cinnamon
⅛ teaspoon salt
4 cups pared and cored thin apple slices
Unbaked pie shell, either homemade or bought
¾ cup packed brown sugar
¾ cup flour
⅓ cup butter

Mix together sugar, cinnamon, salt and apple slices. Arrange in pie shell. Combine brown sugar and flour. Cut in butter with two knives. Sprinkle over apples. Bake at 400 degrees for 30 to 35 minutes. Serve with cream or vanilla ice cream.

Recipe from Edna Pasour White.

Biscuits

2 cups flour
2 teaspoons baking powder
½ teaspoon salt
4 tablespoons shortening
⅔ cup sweet milk

Sift flour, baking powder and salt together. Mix in shortening and add milk to make a soft dough. Knead lightly on a floured board. Roll and cut, not too thin, about ½-inch thick. (You can buy biscuit cutters, or you can use the rim of a glass.) Place in pan and bake 15 or 20 minutes.

Recipe from Tessie Shell.

My mother always called really large biscuits "cat heads." They are best warm, but if you have leftovers, they make great milk toast.

Milk Toast

This was usually eaten at breakfast or supper in the late 1800s and early 1900s. (Not too many people ate breakfast cereal until the companies started sending it home free with schoolchildren.)

Day old bread is best. Open up a biscuit. Spread soft butter on it and put a spoon of white sugar on top of the butter. Sprinkle with cinnamon sugar. Place the biscuit halves on a cookie sheet in the oven under the broiler. Watch so they don't burn. When they are lightly toasted, put them in a cake pan and add about half an inch of warm milk with a little sugar and ½ teaspoon vanilla stirred into the milk. Don't cover the bread. Place the pan back into the oven with medium (350) heat for about 15 minutes or until most of the milk has been absorbed. You don't want the bread too soggy.

Cinnamon Toast

Most people give this their own creative touch. Toast one side of sliced light bread in the oven and turn over. On the untoasted side, spread a mixture of soft butter, cinnamon and sugar. You can use a little brown sugar as well. Put the pan back in the oven and toast until just starting to get a little brown.

Corn Bread (Without Milk)

2 eggs
½ cup cooking oil
1 cup sour cream (not light)
1 cup cream-style corn
1 cup self-rising cornmeal

Mix and bake at 400 degrees for as long as it takes.

Recipe from Elouise Ball Falls.

Crackling Bread

1 quart of cornmeal
1 teaspoon of baking soda
Big pinch salt
1 pint of buttermilk
1 pint of brown cracklings
Warm water

Mix the cornmeal, baking soda and salt and add the buttermilk to make a dough. Crush the cracklings with a rolling pin, heat them and stir them into the dough, which must be thick enough to mold well (thin with the warm water). Mold the bread with your hands in small oblong pones, about three inches thick, putting the pones as you mold them in hot, well-greased pans. Bake in a hot oven (450 degrees) until brown.

Recipe from Mabel Niven Hoffman.

Fried Corn Bread

Fried corn bread was a staple for the South during the Civil War. These cakes are delicious. Don't have the skillet too hot or with too much grease, or they will burn—just hot enough to brown the cakes nicely on both sides. You may add one egg to this batter if you like. I do this sometimes.

1 cup cornmeal
1 tablespoon flour
1 teaspoon salt
¼ teaspoon baking soda
Buttermilk

Sift first four ingredients together and add enough buttermilk (start with ¼ cup and add more as needed) to make a soft batter. Drop by spoonfuls into a hot greased skillet. Brown nicely on each side. (Much like making pancakes but the batter won't spread out as much.)

Recipe from Leola White Wilson.

HUSH PUPPIES

1 bottle vegetable oil (use enough to fill fryer or pot three to four inches)
¾ cups cornmeal
¼ teaspoon salt
1 teaspoon baking powder
¼ cup water
¼ cup milk

Heat oil to 365 degrees in a deep fryer or large, heavy-bottomed pot (about three or four inches deep). While oil is heating, sift meal, salt and baking powder together. Mix water and milk together and stir into dry ingredients. Let stand for 5 to 10 minutes. Then drop by teaspoonfuls into the hot oil. Fry until brown, about 3 to 5 minutes, removing from oil with a slotted spoon. Makes 12 to 15 hush puppies.

Recipe from Helen Durham.

SOUR MILK WAFFLES

1 egg, beaten lightly
½ teaspoon salt
1½ tablespoons shortening, melted
¼ cup cold water
½ cup sour milk
1 tablespoon sugar
1 cup flour
1 tablespoon baking powder

Combine ingredients and beat batter until smooth. Put in small pitcher and pour or use about four tablespoons for each waffle. Makes four waffles.

Recipe from Ruby Costner, daughter of Hersilia Pasour Costner.

Oyster Stew

It was traditional to serve oyster stew on Christmas Eve. This recipe is very old.

1 pint fresh oysters
2 rounding tablespoons butter
1 quart sweet milk
1 teaspoon salt
Pepper

Drain oysters. Put butter into saucepan. When melted add oysters and cook until edges curl. Have milk scalding. As soon as oysters' edges curl, add salt and pepper. Pour on the hot milk. Serve at once.

Recipe from May Webb Shuford.

Cream of Tomato Soup

3 tablespoons butter
3 tablespoons flour
1 teaspoon salt
3 cups milk
3 cups tomatoes, strained
1 teaspoon onion juice
½ teaspoon baking soda

Melt butter in pot and add flour and salt and stir until smooth. Keep stirring and slowly add the milk and cook, stirring occasionally, until thickened. Heat the strained tomatoes and onion juice in a separate pan. Add baking soda to them. Then pour this into the hot milk mixture and stir to mix well.

Recipe from Pearl Jenkins Summey.

VEGETABLE SANDWICH FILLING

1 envelope unflavored gelatin
¼ cup milk
¼ cup mayonnaise or more, to taste
1 (8-ounce) package cream cheese at room temperature
¼ cup chopped nuts
1 tablespoon lemon juice
¼ cup chopped celery
¼ cup chopped onion
¼ cup grated carrots
¼ cup grated cucumber
¼ cup chopped green pepper
10 slices of bread, whole wheat is good

Dissolve gelatin in milk. Add mayonnaise and cream cheese. Add nuts, lemon juice and vegetables. Mix well. Spread on bread. Will make five sandwiches.

Recipe from Sara Fogle Beaty, president of the Dallas Woman's Club, 2008–2012.

PEANUT-APPLE BUTTER SANDWICH

These pair well with Cream of Tomato Soup (page 145).

½ cup peanut butter
⅔ cup apple butter
1 teaspoon honey (or maple syrup)

Mix all ingredients together until well blended. Store covered in refrigerator.

Recipe from Geraldine Ballew Cloninger.

Many people wait with great anticipation for the first tomato sandwich of the season. *Courtesy of local artist Randall Jones.*

Fruit or Vegetable Sandwiches

Fruit and vegetable sandwiches have always been popular in the South. When I was young, boys and girls took them to school for lunch. Most are made the same way. Just put some mayonnaise (Duke's is preferable) on your sliced bread and then put your fruit or vegetable on it. Here are four favorites:

BANANA SANDWICHES

To make banana sandwiches, slice a banana into ¼- to ½-inch pieces and arrange slices on prepared (spread with mayonnaise or peanut butter) bread. You can add raisins as well.

RAISIN SANDWICHES

For raisin sandwiches, sprinkle a handful of raisins on the prepared bread slices. You can substitute peanut butter for the mayonnaise.

GREEN PEPPER SANDWICHES

For green pepper sandwiches, chop a green bell pepper and arrange diced pieces on your bread. This is a tradition with fried chicken at a picnic or family reunion, especially the Pasour reunions.

TOMATO SANDWICHES

For tomato sandwiches, a particular favorite, slice a fresh tomato and layer it onto the mayonnaise-prepared bread. Even the North Carolina state legislature and some churches serve "tomato sandwich suppers" during the summer.

Sour Kraut

1 quart chopped cabbage
1 ½ teaspoon salt
1 ½ teaspoon sugar

Crush chopped cabbage until slightly wilted and pack loosely in sterilized jars. Add salt and sugar. Fill to within ½ inch of top with boiling water and seal.

Recipe from Margaret Blalock Dixon.

Chicken Salad

1 fat hen
6 or 8 boiled eggs, diced
3 cups celery, diced
¼ to ½ cup mayonnaise (preferably Duke's)
Salt and pepper

Cook and debone the hen. Cut with scissors in small pieces. Mix chicken, eggs and celery together and add mayonnaise, enough to hold the ingredients together. Add salt and pepper to taste.

Recipe from Allie White Hoffman.

Five Things Salad

1 bag miniature marshmallows
1 can each crushed pineapple, mandarin oranges and angel flake coconut
1 cup sour cream (Cool Whip may be used)

Drain fruits and mix all ingredients together. Chill.

Recipe from Hilda Stowe Queen.

Barbecue Slaw

½ medium head cabbage
3 teaspoons vinegar
Salt and pepper to taste
¼ cup sugar
2 tablespoons mustard
½ cup ketchup
4 tablespoons mayonnaise
3 tablespoons hot sauce, such as Texas Pete
½ a bottle of steak sauce, such as Heinz 57 Sauce

Chop the cabbage and put it in a bowl. Chill while you prepare the other ingredients. Put all of the remaining ingredients in a large mixing bowl and mix well. Add the cabbage and stir until well coated. Let chill for ½ hour before using.

Recipe of Thelma Cloninger.

CORN SOUFFLÉ

2 eggs, separated
1 tablespoon butter
2 tablespoon flour
1 cup milk
1 large can corn
1½ teaspoons salt
Pinch pepper

Beat egg yolks in a small mixing bowl and set aside. In a separate bowl, or stand mixer, beat whites on high until they stiffen and look dry, and reserve. Meanwhile, melt butter in a large saucepan. Add flour and cook stirring for 2 or 3 minutes. Then, gradually add milk and bring to a boil, stirring continually. Add ¼ to ½ cup of the hot milk mixture to the beaten yolks and stir before adding them to the saucepan (to avoid cooking eggs). Remove from heat. Add corn and seasonings and carefully stir in the stiff egg whites. Put into buttered baking dish and bake at 375 degrees for 25 to 30 minutes.

Recipe from Maria Maness Pasour. Mrs. Pasour was the home economics teacher in the high school.

FRIED GREEN TOMATOES

6 green tomatoes
2 eggs, beaten
1 cup bread crumbs
Salt and pepper
2 or 3 tablespoons corn oil (if frying)

Wash tomatoes and then slice into thick slices. Dip slices into beaten egg and then into the bread crumbs. Dip again into eggs and crumbs. Salt and pepper to taste. Fry tomatoes in hot corn oil. Alternatively, you can broil or bake in a 400-degree oven until crumbs are brown.

Recipe from Jean Durham Harris, granddaughter of "Littlel Denie Lewis" (Mary Modina Lewis Durham).

Squash Casserole with Sour Cream

2 pounds squash, cooked and drained
1 can cream mushroom soup
2 eggs
½ cup cracker crumbs
1½ teaspoon onion flakes
1 cup sour cream
½ cup grated cheese

Grease casserole dish and layer squash. Then mix together remaining ingredients and pour over squash. Top with grated cheese and bake for 45 minutes at 350 degrees.

Recipe from Nancy Rhyne Fogle. Mrs. Fogle used to let the high school kids have sock hops in her living room—push back the furniture, roll up the rug, turn up the music, take off your shoes and dance.

Tomato Side Dish

Make a great tomato side dish with sliced tomatoes just picked from the garden, onions sliced thin and cucumbers. Marinate for 15 minutes in vinegar, oil, salt, pepper and a pinch of sugar. Arrange on serving plate.

Recipe from Clarence Thornburg.

BARBECUED PORK

4 to 5 pounds Boston butt or fresh ham
1 large onion, chopped
3 tablespoons brown sugar
3 tablespoons dry mustard
¼ teaspoon red pepper
¼ teaspoon black pepper
1 cup vinegar
1½ cups water
½ cup ketchup
½ cup Worcestershire sauce
1 tablespoon salt

Put meat in roaster or slow cooker. Mix onion, sugar, mustard, red pepper, black pepper, vinegar, water, ketchup, Worcestershire sauce and salt and pour over meat. Cover roaster and cook at 350 degrees for 5 to 6 hours, or until meat is tender and falls from the bone. Remove fat and skin and chop meat. Heat in sauce.

Recipe from Rebecca Rhyne. An unbelievable woman—on her ninetieth birthday, Rebecca bought a new car and got her driver's license renewed—she also volunteers for many worthy organizations in town.

CHICKEN PIE

1 whole chicken
8 hardboiled eggs
Homemade or store-bought pastry dough
Hot chicken broth

Cook chicken until thoroughly done, about 1 hour. Remove from bones and cut in pieces about two inches long. Place a layer of chicken and sliced boiled eggs in a casserole dish. Cover with strips of pastry. Then add another layer of chicken and boiled eggs. Cover with pastry. Add hot broth to this. Let broth more than cover the layers as pastry will thicken it. Cook in moderate (350-degree) oven.

Recipe from Adelaide McLurd Spargo.

How to Cure Fresh Ham

FOR EVERY 20 POUNDS OF MEAT USE:
1 pint salt
1 tablespoon black pepper
1 tablespoon red pepper
2 tablespoons brown sugar

Combine ingredients and rub into meat thoroughly. Then, wrap the meat in brown paper, put it in bags and hang up at once.

Recipe from Mrs. Fred Stowe.

Fried Chicken and Gravy

1 whole chicken
½ cup flour
½ teaspoon salt
¼ teaspoon pepper
2 or 3 tablespoons vegetable oil

FOR GRAVY:
2 or 3 tablespoons flour
1 cup water or milk
Salt and pepper to taste

Clean, dress and cut chicken in pieces. Place in pan of cold water. Place flour, salt and pepper in a dish. Take the chicken from the water and without drying dredge in the flour. Heat oil in a large skillet. Place chicken pieces in oil and fry on both sides until a golden brown. Do not cover with lid, but cook at moderate heat until tender.

To make gravy, remove the chicken from the pan and pour off some of the fat, leaving around two tablespoons in the pan. Place flour in the fat and brown. Add water or milk and cook for a short time. Add salt and pepper.

Recipe from Adelaide McLurd Spargo.

Sausage Savory with Rice

2 tablespoons fat (Crisco or butter were often used)
1 chopped onion
1 cup water
1 cup uncooked rice
1 can tomatoes
1 cup celery
½ pound sausage
1 tablespoon salt

Heat fat (butter/oil). Add chopped onion and water. Cook until golden. Add uncooked rice, tomatoes, celery, sausage and salt. Let simmer for 30 minutes.

Recipe from Pauline Costner Rhyne.

Black Walnut Pound Cake

The first thing the pioneers planted by their new home was usually a black walnut tree. If you are trying to find an old homestead, look for a black walnut tree.

½ cup Crisco
2 sticks butter
1 (16-ounce) box light brown sugar
1 cup sugar
5 eggs
1 teaspoon vanilla
3 cups flour
½ teaspoon baking powder
½ teaspoon salt
1 cup milk
1 cup chopped black walnuts

Cream Crisco, butter and sugars. Add eggs, one at a time, and vanilla. Combine flour, baking powder and salt in a mixing bowl. Add dry ingredients to wet mixture, alternating with milk, until all is incorporated. Stir in nuts. Bake in prepared pan at 325 degrees for 1½ hours.

Recipe from Polly Clemmer.

Fried Apple Pies

Carl Lee Hoffman made these pies for his children.

¼ pound dried apples
½ cup sugar
1 teaspoon butter
1 teaspoon apple pie spice
Canned biscuits or homemade biscuit dough
Crisco, for frying

Cook apples with a little water until soft. Add sugar, butter and apple pie spice. Combine two biscuits and roll out the dough. On half of rolled-out dough put some of the apple mixture. Fold dough over and mesh edges with a fork; prick the top. Fry in frying pan with Crisco.

Recipe from Allie White Hoffman.

Banana Pudding

1 large vanilla instant pudding mix
1 to 1½ cups cold milk
1 can sweetened condensed milk
1 (9-ounce) carton Cool Whip (or whipped cream)
8 ripe bananas
1 box vanilla wafers

Combine pudding mix and milk and stir until well combined. Then add sweetened condensed milk and stir. Refrigerate until set (about 10 minutes). Add a large spoonful or two of Cool Whip to the pudding and mix. In a two-quart dish lay alternating layers of wafers, bananas and pudding until ingredients are gone, ending with pudding on top. Top with the remaining Cool Whip. Chill several hours or overnight (best overnight, if you can wait that long).

Recipe from Mary Ellen Thornburg.

PULLED MINTS

2 cups sugar
⅛ pound (2 tablespoons) butter
1 cup boiling water
24 drops peppermint extract

Put sugar, butter and water in a saucepan and stir until sugar is thoroughly dissolved. Place on stove and boil rapidly, without stirring, until mixture hardens in water. Pour on slightly greased marble slab to cool. Add peppermint extract when cool. Pull and cut into desired shape with scissors. When the crust begins to form on mints put into an air-tight container to harden.

Recipe from Corinne Puett.

Pulled mints were always served at teas and receptions. My mother also made them for special Dallas Readers' Book Club meetings and Woman's Club meetings. The Dallas Readers' Book Club had its beginning when my mother's family lived in the White House Hotel next door to Beth Friday's home. As my mother told it, Allie White, the youngest in the family, got sick and had to miss most of a year of school. To entertain her, my mother, Leola White, Beth Friday, Madge Houser and Alena Rhyne began a book club. There wasn't a library in Dallas at the time. (Later, the Dallas Library was in the courthouse, with Wilma "Woots" Lineberger Knoles as Dallas's first librarian, before a library was built on West Main Street.) That book club, with many different members, met every month for almost eighty years and outlived all of its charter members.

Red Plum Meringues

This was my mother's "go to" recipe for something "fancy."

FOR MERINGUES:

3 egg whites
¼ teaspoon cream of tartar
¾ cups sugar
Unglazed paper

FOR PLUM FILLING:

2 cups sliced, pitted fresh red plums
⅔ cups water
3 tablespoons quick-cooking tapioca
¾ cups sugar
¼ teaspoon salt

Meringues (be sure to make on a day when the air is dry): Beat whites until foamy throughout. Add cream of tartar and beat until stiff. Add sugar, 2 tablespoons at a time, beating after each addition, until sugar is blended. Then, continue beating until meringues will stand in very stiff peaks. Using a spoon or pastry tube, shape meringue into six rounds on unglazed paper. (I cut a brown paper bag open and use it.) Make each about 4 inches in diameter and about 1½ inches high. Make a depression with spoon in center of each. Bake in slow oven (275 degrees) 45 to 50 minutes. Cool and remove paper. Store in air-tight place.

Plum filling: Mix plums and ⅓ cup of water in a saucepan and bring to a boil. Add quick-cooking tapioca, sugar, salt and remaining ⅓ cup water. Cook and stir over medium heat until mixture comes to boil. Set aside to cool. Chill. Serve in meringue shells. Garnish with slices of plum and mint leaves if desired.

Recipe from Kitty White Thornburg.

SNOW CREAM

We always waited with anticipation for the first heavy snow. You put a stainless-steel mixing bowl outside, or in the freezer, to get it very cold. Then you made up a mixture of canned evaporated milk, sugar and vanilla (to taste, no real recipe) stirring until the sugar was dissolved and put it in the refrigerator. Quickly, you took the cold stainless-steel bowl, raced outside and carefully scooped up a bowlful of clean, light, fluffy snow. Add the liquid slowly and stir so the snow doesn't melt. Enjoy immediately before it's gone. There's never enough.

Recipe from the way I remember it. Courtesy of the author.

REFRIGERATOR ICE CREAM

3 eggs
1 cup sugar
3 cups milk, scalded
½ cup whipped cream
Fruit or flavoring according to preference

Beat eggs thoroughly. Add sugar and blend well. Slowly, add scalded milk. Place mixture in a double boiler and cook, stirring constantly, to make a soft custard. Remove from heat and let stand until cool. Put in tray in refrigerator and when about half frozen stir well until smooth. Add ½ cup whipped cream. Return to refrigerator and freeze. Any flavoring or fruit may be used.

Recipe of Mrs. Cornelius White.

Muscadine Wine

Many people made homemade wine, and some still do.

For every gallon of muscadine grapes, use 1 quart of water.

Mash the grapes well and stir while pouring in water. Let stand 24 hours, and then separate the juice from the skins and pulp using a strainer. For every gallon of juice, add three pounds of sugar. Cover and let stand three days; then if there is a scum on it, remove scum, and let juice stand three more weeks. Then bottle.

Recipe from Lucile Tatum, 4-H leader and extension service director, and much more.

There was a time before Gaston County was known for its textile mills, when it was known for its moonshine and sometimes called "The Banner Corn Whiskey County." When I was very young, I heard old stories of a family or two who used to have pipes hooked right up to their kitchen sink. One, they had for running water, and the other was for moonshine. Dallas was a dry town up until recent years, and some people took it upon themselves to make their own.

Pecan Pie

1 cup corn syrup
3 eggs, beaten lightly
¼ cup melted butter
1 cup pecan halves
Premade or store-bought rich pastry dough
1 teaspoon vanilla
½ cup sugar

Combine first three ingredients. Add pecans. Line pie pan with pastry, fluting edges. Fill with mixture. Bake in 425-degree oven for 10 minutes. Then lower temperature to 350, and bake 30 minutes or until filling is firm.

Recipe of Bettie Pasour Holland.

LIGHT OPERA CREAMS

1 cup sugar
1 cup milk
¾ cup cream
1 tablespoon light corn syrup
⅛ teaspoon salt
1 teaspoon vanilla
1 cup pecans, finely chopped

Combine first 5 ingredients. Cook, stirring constantly until it reaches the soft ball stage (234–236 degrees) on a candy thermometer. Remove from stove; cool without stirring until lukewarm (110 degrees). Add vanilla, beat until creamy. Takes about 15 minutes. Add finely chopped pecans. Drop by spoonfuls on buttered pan. They need to cool and dry out and harden a little until they will come up easily in your hand. Then, enjoy!

Recipe from Kitty White Thornburg.

WATERMELON RIND PICKLES
YOU MAY ONLY WANT TO MAKE HALF A RECIPE.

7 pounds watermelon rind
1 gallon lime water (recipe included)
7 pounds sugar
2 heaping tablespoons ground ginger
3 tablespoons allspice
2 cinnamon sticks
(Spices may vary to suit taste)
2 pints vinegar

Peel and cut rind into serving pieces. (To peel the rind, you cut off the green part, like peeling an apple, and discard. Cut the white part into chunks about an inch square, but this is not precise. The white part is all you use for pickles.) Soak overnight in lime water. In the morning, wash rind in cold water three times. Cook in clear water until tender. Drain well. Meanwhile, combine sugar, spices and vinegar in a medium saucepan and heat to make a syrup. Cook syrup until thick and clear. Place the rind in a large bowl and pour pickling liquid over it. Can in hot, sterilized jars. (Very good if you wrap bacon around a chunk and bake until the bacon is done. Sometimes served at parties.)

Recipe from Leola White Wilson.

Lime Water Recipe

1 gallon water
1 tablespoon lime
1 teaspoon alum powder

Combine ingredients, stirring to dissolve powder.

Taffy Candy

3 cups sugar
¾ cup water
3 tablespoons strong vinegar
Butter size of a walnut (1 tablespoon)
1 teaspoon vanilla

Dissolve sugar in water. Add vinegar and butter. Cook until mixture hardens in water. Pour on greased pans. Add vanilla. When cool enough, pull until white. Break with a knife.

Recipe from Jessie Shuford Summey. Jessie Summey had an antique store by her house.

Lazy Day Cherry Cobbler

1 stick butter, melted
1 cup self-rising flour
¾ cup milk
1½ cups sugar, divided
1 medium can water-packed cherries (not drained)

Put melted butter in a deep baking dish. Beat flour, milk and 1 cup of the sugar to a smooth batter. Pour over melted butter but do not stir. Empty cherries and juice over batter and sprinkle with remaining ½ cup sugar. Bake at 350 degrees for 30 minutes.

Recipe of Coleen Cloninger Peeler. Coleen Cloninger was the first female mayor of Dallas.

Women of the Church group gathered on the steps of the old Lutheran church around 1936. *Front row, left to right*: Edessa Wilson, Lola Cloninger, Angie Lineberger, Ola Hoffman, Nancy Fogle, Desiree Thornburg, Allie Hoffman and Laura Mae Hoffman; *second row*: Madge Houser, Mary Frank Clemmer, Rean Rhyne, Mabel Rudisill, Mrs. Whisenant or Mattie Hoffman, Lena Edison, Ines Gribble, Nellie Clemmer (holding Wayne Ann Clemmer) and Carrie Lineberger; *third row*: Gather McAllister, Pearl Summey, Mary Harwell, Bulah Rhyne and Bryte Pasour; *back row*: Essie Stowe, Addie Pasour, Kitty White Thornburg and Maude Hoffman. *Courtesy of Holy Communion Lutheran Church.*

The Women of the Church at Holy Communion Lutheran Church was a very active group.[112] Many of the women were members of both the Woman's Club and the church group. Some of the recipes are from these talented people.

ANOTHER STORY FROM MY DAD

My dad used to tell of a neighbor being invited out to eat at someone's home, an unusual occurrence for the neighbor. At the end of the meal, he wasn't sure exactly what to say to the hostess, so he tried:

"Mighty good! Mighty good! What there was of it!"

Then, he thought that didn't sound quite right, so he tried again:

"Good enough for anybody, such as it 'tis!

PART IV

GOOD TIMES AND GOOD PEOPLE

10
STORIES OF OLD TIMES

Clarence Thornburg's Story (1898–1989)

From His 1972 Manuscript

This was written in response to my request to "tell me about your childhood." More than half of it is about Cherryville, where he lived from the age of five to fourteen.

> *I was born three and half miles northwest of Dallas, Gaston County, North Carolina, on January 2, 1898.* [He was the son of D.S. Thornburg, a grandson of L.A. Thornburg and born in the L.A. Thornburg house.] *My father worked at the family sawmill on Little Long Creek about five hundred yards from our house. Our house was built of Number 1 heart pine, and it was said that it did not have a knot in it.*
>
> *My earliest recollections were the trips to the millpond with mama above the sawmill* [and] *playing with Polie and Worth Thornburg in our yard. I also remember playing with Charlie Friday's baby daughter and Uncle Jim Falls, who stuttered. The Fridays and Uncle Jim were black, but I never knew the difference. We all were friends and just played together.* [Charlie Friday had a home on Friday Park Road in Dallas and each Fourth of July gave a celebration with fried chicken and

homemade ice cream. The home is no longer there, but Friday Baptist Church is.] *I also remember Dad riding his old-school penny-farthing bicycle* [the kind with the large wheel in front] *to Gastonia every day going to a business school to learn bookkeeping and shorthand in preparation for a job in Cherryville with the Gaston Manufacturing Company for the sum of thirty dollars a month. We moved to Cherryville when I was five years old with my family and two sisters. I started to school the next fall. I was in Mrs. Wilson's room. Boy, was I scared! The next year, we moved to a new house near the mill in the next block to Uncle Polie Rhodes; his children, Coralee, Paul, Ruth, Elsie and Edna, and me and my sisters played all over town. After three years, Uncle Polie's family moved to Lincolnton* [where D.P. "Polie" Rhodes became a Lincoln County commissioner and owned Rhodes Manufacturing Company], *and George Huss moved into their house. We still had playmates in Alvia, Loy and Georgia. A year or so later, the Husses bought the first automobile in town, an old Reo with a gate in the back and seats on each side. Loy and I were the envy of the kids in town, for we rode about everywhere it went.*

My school years were uneventful. My history and arithmetic grades were always good.

In 1910, Dad was appointed postmaster at Cherryville with an increase in pay, but by that time, he and mama had six children. I don't see how we lived. I began to sell the Grit *and also the* Saturday Evening Post *on the weekends. Maybe I would make two dollars a week. About the same time I got a job with Claude Mauney making mortar and hauling bricks for him to lay. He paid me twenty-five cents a day for ten or twelve hours of work. The next job I had was making mortar and hauling brick to three masons on Frank Carpenter's Café. Now it takes three or four men to do the same job.* [Clarence was twelve. All money he made went to help the family.]

In 1914, we moved back to the farm [L.A. Thornburg's farm in Dallas Township]. *I went to the high school in Dallas in the Old Gaston College Building and the Farm Life School held in the courthouse. I played on the first basketball team the school had. In fact, the first one I ever saw. I never was athletic. I would rather fish and hunt. High school was uneventful. I finished in 1917 in a class of three boys and four girls.*

I taught school in 1917 at Pisgah, a two-teacher school. During the summer of 1918, I worked at Camp Lee and Camp Eustis near Newport News, Virginia, for the unheard of sum of five dollars a day. By September, I had registered for the draft [for World War I] *and had decided to volunteer for the Students' Army Training Corps. I spent several months drilling. I was a corporal. After being discharged, I taught at Catawba, North Carolina, for the term.*

My Father's Story

My father was a teacher for two years, a general contractor for forty-three years and a farmer all of his life. My earliest memories are of riding on the back of the mule while he ploughed the fields in the bottoms, of playing in the corn crib and of him making molasses on the hill. He built stores in Detroit and military

A 1908 *Eagle* newspaper photograph of Clarence and Winnie Thornburg's fourth grade class. Students on steps are (front row, from left to right) Guy Sipe, Joe Chapman, Brice Gates, Steele Allran, Floyd Mauney, Clarence Thornburg and Dewey Dellinger. In the second row are (left to right) Eden Foreman, Willie Ballard, Monroe Carpenter, Albert Kale, Eubern Quinn, Victor Stroupe, Virgil Lingerfelt and Jesse Vandyke. In the third row are (left to right) Annie Lee Craft, unknown, Madge Summitt, Miss Lucy Kiser (teacher), Grace Kohn, Eugenia Straussell, Myrtle Crowder and Connie Ballard. And in the fourth row are Pearl Beam, Lucille Jones, Mildred Farris, Winnie Thornburg and Carrie Howell. *Courtesy of the Cherryville Museum of History.*

housing in Panama. Then, he was back home building stores, restaurants, churches and homes in Dallas's and Gastonia's historic districts. He built the old Woolworth Dime Store, the North Carolina Orthopedic Hospital and R.O.'s Barbecue, Holy Communion's fellowship hall and the parsonage. His general contractor's office was in the Hoffman House Hotel. He was active in the church at Holy Communion and in the community as treasurer for the volunteer fire department for twenty years. He was also a big teaser. Wilma Ratchford Craig, *Gaston County Historical Bulletin* editor, grew up on a farm near the Thornburg farm and wrote a poem, "Mr. C.O.," about my dad. He called her one of "Crown's boys" because she did all the farm work a son would do, and then some. My dad said that at Christmas, they got a stocking with oranges, nuts and a few pieces of candy and maybe a small gift. They burned their Christmas tree in a bonfire at midnight on New Year's Eve, an old German tradition, and sang "Auld Lang Syne," a Scottish poem written by Robert Burns. The "New Year's Shooters" from Cherryville came to Dallas Township with their muskets to shoot in the New Year, and most people ate hog jowl or ham hock for health, collard greens for wealth and black-eyed peas for good luck on New Year's Day. Then they sopped up their pot likker with corn bread.

Kitty White Thornburg's Story (1903–1998)

I asked my mother to also write something about when she was young. She wrote about Costner School.

In 1957, Allie White Hoffman, chairman of the Gaston County Educational Heritage Centennial Pageant and Centennial Book, asked her sister Kitty White Thornburg to write the history of the Costner School for the Centennial Book. They were great-granddaughters of Valentine Costner. As children, they had lived next door to the school when it was located on the land given by Peter P. Costner "across the creek on the hill." (I grew up in the same house as they did, and many times I walked into the woods beside our house and saw the bricks from the old school. The house was built by my grandfather and great-grandfather White.) My mother attended the Costner School before it was moved to its present location, and then she attended the new school. She taught at Tryon in the 1920s, Costner in the 1930s to '40s, Dallas in the 1940s to '60s, Carr in the 1960s and other schools, making it forty-two years in Gaston County. The following is the history of Costner School as my mother wrote it:

OLD-FASHIONED STICKIES

1 cup flour
⅛ teaspoon baking soda
¼ teaspoon baking powder
¼ teaspoon salt
2 tablespoons shortening
⅓ cup milk
¼ cup melted butter, ¼ cup sugar and 2 tablespoons cinnamon, adjusted to taste

Combine flour, soda, baking powder and salt. Cut in the shortening and mix. Add the milk, making a dough. Roll out thin and spread with melted butter, sugar and cinnamon. Roll up as jellyroll. Slice into pieces and place on greased pan. Bake at 400 for 8 to 10 minutes.

Kitty White Thornburg's recipe.

Costner School had its beginning in 1830 in a little one-room log house [in the] *back of where Antioch Church is now. Because of a lack of water, it was thought advisable to move the school. Land was given for the new school by Valentine Costner. It was moved to near Costner Spring so the school could use water from the spring and have adequate water for its needs. The school was then called Costner School.* [Costner Spring was located near the bridge over Little Long Creek on Ashebrook Park Road. Many times, I have carried water from that spring to my home on the farm where I grew up. The well house and rail fence are no longer there, nor is the Ralph Costner home. Bess Costner and Ralph Costner were brother and sister and my mother's cousins.]

The building was a one-room log building with a wood floor. A big fireplace was at one end of the building. The seats were benches made of slabs. Across the back of the room was a long desk where the pupils could go to write their copy books. The Blue Back Speller *was used, of course, and the older pupils learned to cipher.*

About a mile down Little Long Creek was a sawmill pond. [This is the same sawmill pond on the L.A. Thornburg page and in Clarence Thornburg's Story.] *The water backed up the creek until it was quite full near the schoolhouse, and the bottoms nearby were covered with large puddles of water. In wintertime, the pond and the water in the bottoms stayed frozen quite a bit of the time. Sometimes, the pond was frozen over for as much as six weeks at a time. The children had a great time skating in the bottoms near the school.*

Mr. Peter P. Costner, son of Valentine Costner, gave the school land "across the creek on the hill" for a new school building after the old one had burned. The new building was almost [just] *like the old one.*

The following are some of the early teachers: Mr. Caleb Pasour, Mr. Peter Marshall Rhyne, Mr. Gideon Gamble, Mr. David Robinson, Mr. John Carson, Mr. Claude Holland, Miss Mamie Johnson, Mr. George Holland, Major Lee Bulwinkle, Miss Mollie Thomas, Mr. Gary Rhyne, Preacher Lohr, Mr. Loy Cornwell, Mr. Willie Jenkins, Miss Mary Hager, Reverend Senter and Miss Bess Costner (who also taught at Hardin). Strict discipline was maintained at all times. The rule of the hickory stick was prevalent.

About the years 1910–12, Costner School was moved to its present location. St. Peter's Lutheran Church, which was no longer in use as a church, was moved from below Antioch Church to the present Costner School grounds. Costner then became a three-teacher school. Some of the children came from the old Jenkins School, which had disbanded.

Jenkins School had been a one-room log school that had been in existence for quite a long time. Many of our older citizens still held cherished memories of their school days at the old Jenkins School house. The Jenkins School House is where my mother [Edna Pasour White, daughter of Simon Peter Pasour] *went to school. She recalled how the girls would square dance at recess time while one or more made the music with their mouths and another called. Or perhaps the boys stopped playing Bull Pen and joined the girls in the dance. Then, one of the boys would play his harp for the dance. Many of the teachers previously named as having taught at Costner's had also taught at the Jenkins School House. To this list I would add a few more: Mr. Will Davenport, Miss Lizzie Clemmer, Miss Julia Clemmer and Miss Maggie Gamble. Some teachers after Costner's was moved to its present location were Miss Alice Huss, Miss Mary Rudisill, Miss Mae Webb, Miss Cora Lee Rhodes, Miss Mary Guffey, Mr. John Rutledge, Mr. Gus Kiser, Mrs. Kitty White Thornburg, Miss Winnie*

Caramel Icing

One of my favorite recipes my mother made when I was young (and always at Christmas—she made five cakes every Christmas) was caramel cake.

2 (1-pound) boxes light brown sugar
15 tablespoons evaporated milk
¼ teaspoon salt
½ pound (2 sticks) butter
1 teaspoon baking powder
2 teaspoons vanilla

Combine sugar, milk and salt in a medium saucepan and blend thoroughly. Add butter and bring to a boil; boil for three minutes after mixture comes to a rolling boil. Meanwhile, fill a pan with cold water and place a mixing bowl in it. Remove caramel mixture from heat and stir in baking powder and vanilla. Pour into prepared mixing bowl and beat until mixture reaches spreading consistency. If mixture gets too hard, add 1 teaspoon water; repeat if necessary. Never take your hand off the spoon from the time you start this icing until it is ready to spread on the cake. (She used a 1, 2, 3, 4 Cake recipe [page 53] for caramel cake, and if she wanted the cake especially white, she put in an extra egg white.)

Recipe from Kitty White Thornburg.

Thornburg, Miss Grace Rhyne, Miss Mary Ellen Thornburg and Miss Lillian Lineberger.

Back in the early days, the families were large, and all the children went to the same school and walked to get there. One of the larger children carried the picnic basket (that is what it was), for at noon, each family would gather in a group, open the basket and have a picnic. There would be pies, perhaps three stacked on top of one another, baked sweet potatoes, ham biscuits, or other meat, and stickies.

A third grade class at Dallas Elementary School in 1950 standing on the side door's steps. *From left to right, front row*: Alice Kincaid, Edward Snyder, Jerry Fogle, Johnny Huss, Lewis Bowman and Linda Parish; *second row*: Barbara Tanner, Emma Snyder, unknown, Linda Cloninger, Lavinia McClure and Linda Holloway; *third row*: unknown, Ronald Mobley, Bennie Gail Cloninger, Vesta Jones and unknown; *fourth row*: Betty Faye Jenkins, Kenny Watson, Michael Atkins, unknown and unknown; *fifth row*: Marie Lineberger, J.D. Arrendale, Burt Holland, Barry Clemmer, Charles Pasour and Joyce Ledford; *sixth row*: Reid Simms, Brenda Toomey, Joyce Deal, Gayle Walker, Kitty Kay Thornburg, Irving Wix and unknown; *back row*: Judy Clark, unknown, Judy Summey, unknown, Faye Medford, Marvin Kirby and Kitty White Thornburg (teacher). *Courtesy of the Thornburg family.*

My mother told a story of getting a doll for Christmas. She had only one doll. It was considered so valuable and expensive that it was kept on the mantel, and she was not allowed to play with it; she could only look at it. Another story was that every morning, she and her sisters were each given a pillowcase to go pick cotton before breakfast and before school. Everyone had to work hard. It wasn't only the kids in the mills who worked hard. It was everyone.

I have a copy of a Costner class register when my great-grandfather, L.A. Thornburg was on the school board and my grandfather was a student with forty-seven other students in the one-room school. I also remember going to Costner to hear the Carter sisters sing (June Carter Cash).

11
NOTABLE PEOPLE

Some notable men and women who once—some still do—called Dallas home are listed below. They should be mentioned in a book on Dallas. Please add any others you think should be named here. Thank you.

Frederick Hambright (1721–1817): He was a Revolutionary War hero at Kings Mountain and commanded the South Fork Boys after the death of William Chronicle. He signed the Tryon resolves in 1775 and had a farm near Pasour Mountain. (He was an ancestor of mine and maybe yours—he had twenty-two children)

Jacob Costner (circa 1740–1779): He was a Revolutionary War soldier, a county official in Tryon County and a signer of the Tryon Resolves. He died as he and his wife, Elizabeth, were trying to cross the South Fork River in a wagon.

John Fulenwider (1756–1826): The founder of the High Shoals Iron Works was one of the first producers of pig iron by the charcoal process. He was a Revolutionary War patriot who made and gave General Washington a rifle in 1787.[113]

Jesse Holland (1786–1856): Holland was the grantor of the land for the town of Dallas and active in the movement to create Gaston County.

James Hillhouse White (1802–1883): As a North Carolina state representative and senator for Lincoln and Gaston for sixteen years (1842–62), he was a "leader in the struggle to establish Gaston County" and is recognized as a "real founder." Many consider him the "Father of Gaston County." He said the "proudest act of his public life was securing the charter of the Lenoir and Chester Railroad (which became the Carolina and Northwestern, then merged with Southern Railway)."[114]

Moses Rhyne (1812–1892): Active in the county of Gaston and town of Dallas, he established an early textile mill and was recognized as a textile industry pioneer, as well as being a benefactor of old Gaston College.

Eli Pasour (1828–1904): He was the first mayor of Dallas, its sixth postmaster and served in the North Carolina legislature in 1881.

Reverend M.L. Little (1848–1891): A late nineteenth-century educator, president of old Gaston College and Gaston Female College, he was actively engaged in the groundwork for Lenoir College (now Lenoir-Rhyne University).

Cornelious Fisher Gingles (1877–1945): Known for his work in education, Gingles was the first principal of 1922 Rosenwall School built on Spargo Street; the minister at First Baptist Church, Dallas; and an early civil rights leader.

Alfred Lewis "Lee" Bulwinkle (1883–1950): Bulwinkle was a World War I veteran, a teacher at Costner School, lawyer in Dallas and Gastonia, a U.S. congressman from North Carolina for twenty-six years (1921–1950) and the U.S. advisor to the International Civil Aviation Organization.

Bess Puett, MD (1894–1938): Puett was the first female doctor in Gaston County. She went straight from Gaston Female College to medical school in Baltimore without additional schooling, and in 1909 she passed her North Carolina State Medical Boards to become a doctor.

Dr. Karl C. Garrison (1900–1991): Garrison was a professor and author of several well-known and widely used educational psychology books, the most prominent being *Psychology of Human Behavior*.

Dr. William C. Friday (1920–2012): He was the longest-serving president of the University of North Carolina (1956–86). In 1985, he received the

American Council on Education's Distinguished Service Lifetime Award. He was rated the most effective public university president in the nation. The Friday Institute in Chapel Hill is named in honor of Bill and Ida Friday for their contributions to higher education. Governor Bev Perdue praised his work: "His dedication and service to North Carolina and monumental impact on our state cannot be overstated. There has been no person in North Carolina history who more fully exemplified how one individual can, year after year, make a tremendous difference."

George Jaggers (1926–2006): In 1989, he became the first black alderman in Dallas. He also served on the Dallas Rescue Squad for twenty-five years and worked in the Dallas Police Department.

Coleen Cloninger (1926–): As the first female mayor in Gaston County in 1992, she was known for town leadership.

Dr. Clarence O. Thornburg Jr. (1938–1975): As a scientist, he built an atomic clock at MIT and became the research director at the National Company, the first company to build commercial atomic clocks.

David Hoyle (1939–): A North Carolina state senator for eighteen years (1993–2011), he was secretary of the North Carolina Department of Revenue and a member of the Governor's Cabinet. At age twenty-seven, he was mayor of Dallas, and he has served on the board of directors at Lenoir-Rhyne University.

Dr. Eugene Elmore (1942–): Known for his contributions in DNA and cancer research, he is on the faculty of the University of California–Irvine.

Pearl Burris-Floyd (1956–): She was the first black North Carolina representative from Gaston County and served on the Education and Appropriations Committees and as a county commissioner. She is the senior advisor to the State Board of Health and Human Services.

Jeffery S. Whisenant (1961–): He is the executive vice-president and acting president and CEO of Lutheran World Relief in Baltimore, Maryland, an international nonprofit that works to end poverty and injustice around the world by empowering communities to help themselves. He grew up as a member of Holy Communion Lutheran Church.

Dallas has been home to many notable, and noble, citizens who have contributed to our town, county, state and country; may we all continue "to give a good accounting to future generations." There is a tombstone in the old Presbyterian cemetery that says, "Life is a dance. Enjoy it every step of the way." May you do both.

MAKE IT YOURS!

Please use any extra space in this book to record notes on your own family connections and heritage. There is almost always more to the story. I have not been able to tell it all, though I tried. Write down your family tree. Put in ancestors and dates. Tell your history, recipes and memories, and tell the things I didn't. There are some treasures only you know. I welcome your comments and stories. In 1955, Miss Corrine Puett wanted to start such a book, but as far as I know, she never did. She did have all the people signed up to write their parts, but she waited too long. She had asked my mother to write a section about midwives because Mother was a granddaughter of Eliza Costner White, who was a midwife in the Costner community. She asked Madge Houser to write about lawyers because her father was a lawyer. She asked Allie Hoffman to write about schools because she was very active in the school system, and so on, but it never happened. Make this book more valuable to your family. Share your family history with your children and grandchildren so they will know.

NOTES

Introduction

1. Dallas, North Carolina 2010 census, census.gov.
2. Gaston Centennial Program, 11, 16.

Part I

3. Rankin, *Gaston*, 15–25.
4. Eloise Falls, interview with the author: grandmother's tribal beads.
5. Hoffman, "First Medical," 1.
6. www.native-languages.org/ncarolina.htm. For more information on Catawba, visit the Schiele Museum in Gastonia.
7. Rankin, *Gaston*, 15–25.
8. Joara Foundation, Warren Wilson College: www.Exploring joara.org/ Catawba meadow
9. Marino, *Pasour*, 31–7.
10. Hoffman, *Our Kin*, 575.
11. www.lib.unc.edu for oral history project. This source lists the most well-known people from North Carolina.
12. Ehringhaus and Goerch, *North Carolina*, 26–35.
13. Ibid.

14. Ibid.
15. Hoskins, "Levi Coffin."
16. www.ncmarkers.com, Tryon Courthouse, #0-29.
17. Harold Underwood Faulkner, *American Political and Social History* (N.p., 1957), 137.
18. www.ncmarkers.com, Fulenwider, #0-54.
19. Cope and Wellman, *County*, 247.
20. Learn NC, NC Digital History, a program of UNC–Chapel Hill.
21. Wehunt-Black, *Gaston County*, 45.
22. Docsouth.unc.edu/william joseph gaston.
23. Gaston County Centennial Program, 11.
24. Stowe, "Jesse Holland," 3.
25. Cope and Wellman, *County*, 235.
26. Oral History, of Randy Thomason, in-person interview, July 3, 2013.
27. Separk, *Gastonia*, 195.
28. Stowe, "Blacksmith Art," 4.
29. Public laws and resolutions, 1909 session, xxxi.
30. Ragan, "Gastonia's," www.vintagegastonia.com (article fourteen).
31. Cope and Wellman, *County*, 135.
32. Robertson, "Organized Work," 1.
33. Cope and Wellman, *County*, 171–3.
34. Ibid., 229–39.
35. sites.google.com/site/childlabornctextilemills.
36. Gaston Centennial Program, 66–7.
37. Garnet Kimbrell, James Robert Carpenter, Ariel Hoffman, Glenn Garrison Rhyne, Harry Taylor, Cecil Blake, Lawrence Holland Jr., Leroy Heilig, Clarence Groves, Flay Dalton Willis, Ralph H. Rhyne, Zado Thornburg, William Lamar Hunt (from an unpublished list, papers of Allie White Hoffman, may not be complete).
38. Oral History, of Mark Pasour, June 2, 1959.

Part II

39. Oral History, of Randy Thomason, July 5, 2013.
40. Ibid. His company made the brick for Johnson C. Smith University in Charlotte.
41. Craig, Introduction, James William Reid's Diary.
42. Stowe, "Gaston Old Homes," 1.
43. Stowe, "6,000 Federal Troops," 1, 2.
44. Gaston County Heritage Book, Vol. 1, "Campo."

45. Gaston Centennial Program, 111–4.
46. Ibid., 114.
47. Gaston County Library, Gaston County Archives for 1892 and 1899.
48. *Charlotte Observer*, May 26, 1905; *Columbia Star*, May 16, 1905.
49. Brengle, *Architecture*, 122.
50. *Gastonia Gazette*, October 15, 1975.
51. Ragan, *Ragans*, 99; *Gastonia Gazette*, January 1, 1998.
52. Lewis, "Gardens," 4.
53. www.gastoncountymuseum.org
54. Annual reports, December 1848 and December 1892; Annual report of the Carolina & Northwestern Railroad, 18.
55. The Dallas Courthouse burned in 1874. Records are online from Princeton University and from the North Carolina General Assembly.
56. Cope and Wellman, *County*, 135.
57. Oral History, of Peggy Hoffman Cearley, July 3, 2013.
58. Gaston Centennial Program, 112.
59. Oral History, of Peggy Hoffman Cearley.
60. Information is from Madge White Houser's writings and my mother's stories.
61. Oral History, of Beth Friday in 1957.
62. Dr. Friday has responded to his home county on a number of occasions to provide his help.
63. Stowe, "History," 3.
64. Wehunt-Black, *Gaston County*, 102–3.
65. Sherrill, *Annals*.
66. www.hollandfamilyresearchers.us/resource center, American Genealogical Research Institute.
67. Gaston Centennial Program, 11.
68. *Gaston County Historical Society Bulletin* (July 1955 and December 1960).
69. *Gastonia Gazette*, "Gaston County's First Court Organized February 1847, (February 3, 1947), 2.
70. Lewis, "Gardens," 4.
71. Hoffman, "First Medical," 2.
72. Oral History, by Edna White, 1955.
73. Oral History, by Hilda Queen in 2010.
74. Gaston County Historical Society, Lewis, "Gardens," 4.
75. Oral History, of Clarence O. Thornburg, Jan. 2, 1972
76. *Gaston County Historical Society Bulletin* (December 1968).
77. Mentioned in his obituary in the *Charlotte Observer* on October 12, 2012.

78. This was the house (on Lot 7) that stood between the Eli Pasour house and the Roberts-Lewis house on the Square. The families gathered are the children and grandchildren of L.A. Thornburg.
79. Rankin, *Gaston*, 48.
80. Oral History, of Peggy Hoffman Cearly, July 3, 2013.
81. Hoffman, *Our Kin*, 75.
82. Branson's NC Business Directory, 1890.
83. Gaston Centennial Program, 16.
84. Educational Heritage (1957), Mitchell Carr, 38.
85. The 1914 girls basketball team (only part of it is pictured) was made up of students who attended high school in the old college. The only one identified is Winnie Thornburg, standing in the middle.
86. Educational Heritage (1957), Mitchell Carr, "Dallas Schools."
87. Cloninger, "Old Timey Coffins," 4.
88. Gaston County Heritage Book, Vol. 1.
89. Gaston County Educational Heritage (1957), Carr, "Dallas Schools."
90. Mike Baxter, Gaston County Museum of Art and History, "Caroline Shipp," 2010 presentation.
91. Smith, "Dr. Bess," 1,3.
92. Hoffman, *Our Kin*, 367.
93. North Carolina troops registry, Company A, Eleventh Regiment.
94. Reported in the *Charlotte Observer*, 1965.
95. Cope and Wellman, *County*, 68.
96. Houser, "Sketch," 1–3.
97. North Carolina troop registry, Sixteenth Regiment.
98. Cope and Wellman, *County*, 191.
99. Quote from L.A. Thornburg's unpublished account of the war from a seventeen-year-old's point of view, written around the late 1800s and still in the possession of his family.
100. Philip Gerard, "Gettysburg," *North Carolina State Magazine*, April 2013, 57.
101. Robert Carpenter, *Footprints*.
102. North Carolina troops registry, Confederate officer, Thirty-seventh Regiment.
103. Wilson, "Gaston Man's Worth," 1–2.
104. North Carolina troops registry.
105. Carr, "History,"1–3.
106. North Carolina Civil War trail markers along the Catawba River put Stoneman in Lincolnton on April 16, 1865, six days after Appomattox and one day after Abraham Lincoln's death.
107. Herran, *They Married*, 98.

108. National History Day in North Carolina.
109. Gaston County Centennial Program, Madge White Houser, 113.
110. Rankin, *Gaston*, 44.

PART III

111. This is a Pasour family reunion in 1929. Most of the women seated in chairs on the right side of the photograph are daughters of Simon Peter Pasour and Diana Broom Pasour. Those seated on the left side are daughters and a son of David Rufus Pasour and Lavinia Withers Pasour. Other siblings, in-laws, children and grandchildren surround them.
112. A group of women from the congregation standing on the steps of the 1906 Holy Communion Lutheran Church. Many of these were also in the Dallas Woman's Club and contributed recipes.

PART IV

113. Cope and Wellman, *County*, 247.
114. Ibid., 162; Ragan, *Ragans*, 24; Kathy Lawrence, in the *Gastonia Gazette*, wrote that many considered him the "Father of Gaston County"; Cope and Wellman, *County*, 123.

BIBLIOGRAPHY

Newspapers

Charlotte Observer, May 26, 1905, October 12, 2012
Columbia Star, May 16, 1905
Gastonia Gazette, November 16, 1883, October 1, 1907, October 15, 1975, January 1, 1998
Lincolnton Chronicle, March 30, 1848
Monroe Examiner, May 1879
Raleigh News and Observer, April 1846

Church Histories

Dallas Baptist Church, courtesy of Dallas Baptist Church
First United Methodist, courtesy of First United Methodist Church
Holy Communion Lutheran, courtesy of Holy Communion Lutheran
Long Creek Baptist Church, courtesy of Long Creek Baptist Church
Philadelphia Lutheran, courtesy of Philadelphia Lutheran Church

Abernathy, Myrtle, "Facts about Pinhook Mill." *Gaston County Historical Society Bulletin* 7, no. 2 (1961): 3.

Annual Reports of the Board of Railroad Commissioners of NC, 1848–1892. Princeton University Library, Princeton, NJ.

Baxter, Mike. "Caroline Ship." 2010 presentation. Gaston County Museum of Art and History.

Blue, Anthony Dias. *America's Kitchen,* Atlanta, GA: Turner Publishing, 1995.

Brengle, Kim Withers. *The Architectural Heritage of Gaston County NC.* Gastonia, NC: Commercial Printers, 1982.

Carpenter, Robert C. *Carpenters A Plenty*. Baltimore, MD: Gateway Press, 1982.

———. *Footprints in Time*. Mount Holly, NC: Gaston-Lincoln Genealogical Society, 2011.

Carr, Betty. "A History of Philadelphia Lutheran." *Gaston County Historical Society Bulletin* 14, no. 1 (1968): 1–3.

Catawba Tribe: www.native-languages.org/ncarolina.htm. For more information on Catawba, visit the Schiele Museum in Gastonia.

Cearley, Peggy Hoffman. Interview with the author. July 3, 2013.

Child Labor in North Carolina Textile Mills. sites.google.com/site/childlaborncte xtilemills.

Cloninger, Burt. "Old Timey Coffins," *Gaston County Historical Society Bulletin* 21, no. 1 (1975): 4.

Cope, Robert F., and Manly Wade Wellman. *The County of Gaston*. Charlotte, NC: Heritage Printers, 1961.

———. "History Recounted from Early Days." *Gaston County Historical Society Bulletin* 2, no. 4 (1956): 1–4.

Craig, Wilma Ratchford. Introduction to *A Complete 1850 Census of Gaston County NC* by Libby Goodnight, et al. "Cemeteries" and "James William Reid's Diary," Ozark, MS: Yates Publishing Company, 2013.

Editor's Notes. "Branson's NC Business Directory, 1890." *Gaston County Historical Society Bulletin* 2, no. 4 (1956): 3.

Ehringhaus, Mrs. J.C.B., and Mrs. Carl Goerch. *North Carolina Almanac and State Industrial Guide 1950–51*. Raleigh, NC: Almanac Publishing Company, 1950.

Falls, Eloise. Interviews with the author over three separate meetings. June 2013.

Faulkner, Harold Underwood. *American Political and Social History*. New York: Appleton, Century, Croft, 1957.

Friday, Beth. Interview with the author. 1957.

Gaston Centennial Souvenir Program, GCSP. 1946.

Gaston County Educational Heritage, GCEH. 1957.

Gaston County Historical Society Bulletins, GCHSB. 1954–1983.

Gaston County Library, Gaston County Archives for 1892 and 1899.

Gold Mines. Learn NC, NC Digital History, a program of UNC–Chapel Hill.

Goodnight, Libby Wyatt, Linda Adams Bell, and Robert C. Carpenter. *A Complete 1850 Census of Gaston County, NC*. Ozark, MS: Yates Publishing Company, 2013.

Griffin, Sally. *Gaston Remembers, Weaving a Tapestry in Time*. Montgomery, AL: Community Communications, 1994.

Harris, Jean Durham. Interview with the author. August 2013.

Herran, Kathy Neill. *They Married Confederate Officers*. Davidson, NC: Warren Publishing, 1997.

Hoffman, Carl W. "First Medical Practitioners in Gaston." *Gaston County Historical Society Bulletin* 12, no. 1 (1966): 1–2.

Hoffman, L.M. *Our Kin*. Baltimore, MD: Genealogical Publishing Company, 1915.

Holland Family. www.hollandfamilyresearchers.us/resource center. American Genealogical Research Institute.

Hoskins, Mary Catherine. "Levi Coffin: 1798–1877." Documenting the American South. http://docsouth.unc.edu/nc/coffin/bio.html.

Houser, Madge White. "Sketch of the White Family." *Gaston County Historical Society Bulletin* 1, no. 1 (1954): 1–3.

Joara Foundation. Warren Wilson College: www.Exploring joara.org/Catawba meadow

Kelly, C. Brian, and Ingrid Smyer. *Best Little Stories from the Civil War*. Nashville, TN: Cumberland House Publishing, 2010.

Lewis, Carrie Puett. "Gardens of Early Settlers." *Gaston County Historical Society Bulletin* 13, no. 1 (1967): 3.
Library of Congress. American Life Series. memory.loc.gov/ammem/index.html.
Marino, Thomas J. *Pasour, Paysour, Payseur, Paseur, Together…at Last.* Birmingham, AL: Birmingham Publishing Company, 1992.
———. Reproduction of "Costner School, A One-Room Schoolhouse's Original School Register, 1892–1901." Hoover, AL: TJM Enterprises, 1992.
Marker: www.ncmarkers.com, Fulenwider, #0-54.
Marker: www.ncmarkers.com, Tryon Courthouse, #0-29.
Museum brochure. www.gastoncountymuseum.org.
Nixon, Alfred. "The History of Lincoln County." *North Carolina Booklet* 9, no. 3 (January 1910).
North Carolina Civil War trail markers along the Catawba River. www.civilwartrails.org (accessed January 19, 2012)
North Carolina state historical highway markers and descriptions books.
North Carolina troops registry. North Carolina State Archives, Raleigh, NC.
Oral History Project. www.lib.unc.edu. This source lists the most well-known people from North Carolina.
Pasour, Mark. "Oral History." Presentation by Mark Pasour. June 2, 1959.
Powell, William S. *Dictionary of North Carolina Biography II.* Chapel Hill: University of North Carolina Press, 2006.
———. *Encyclopedia of North Carolina.* Chapel Hill: University of North Carolina Press, 2006.
Public laws and resolutions of the State of North Carolina. North Carolina State Archives, Raleigh, NC.
Puett, Minnie Stowe. *History of Gaston County*. Charlotte, NC: Observer Printing House, 1939.
Queen, Hilda Stowe. Interview with the author. 2010.
Ragan, Robert Allison. "Gastonia's Battle for the County Seat." Article fourteen in *Vintage Gastonia.* Gastonia, NC, www.vintagegastonia.com. 2012.
———. *The Ragans of Gastonia 1790–1995.* Charlotte, NC: Heritage, 2010.
Rankin, Richard. *Gaston and Lincoln Sketches*. Gastonia, NC: Pipes & Timbrels Press, 2006.
Recipes courtesy of the Dallas Woman's Club. Cookbooks, 1917, 1947 and 1954.
Robertson Nellie. "The Organized Work of Women in One State." *Journal of Social Forces* 1, no. 1 (January 1919): 1.
Schumann, Marguerite. *Tar Heel Sights: A Guide to North Carolina's Heritage*. Charlotte, NC: East Woods Press, 1983.
Separk, Joseph. *Gastonia and Gaston County Past, Present, and Future.* Kingsport, TN: Kingsport Press, 1936.
Sherrill, William L. *Annals of Lincoln County*. Lincolnton, NC: *Lincoln Times*, 1937. With reprints from the North Carolina House of Commons, *Gastonia Gazette* and others, 1937. (Originally published as newspaper articles in the *Lincoln Times.*)
Smith, Lois. "Doctor Bess Puett Was First Woman Doctor in Gaston." *Gaston County Historical Society Bulletin* 9, no. 1 (1963): 1–3.
Stowe, Dalton. "Blacksmith's Art Becoming Lost Art." *Gaston County Historical Society Bulletin* 2, no. 2 (1956): 4.
———. "Gaston County Historic Courthouse." *Gaston County Historical Society Bulletin* 1, no. 1 (1954): 1–3.

———. "Gaston Old Homes (Jesse Holland's Brick)." *Gaston County Historical Society Bulletin* 5, no. 2 (1959): 1.

———. "History Is Rolled Back 110 Years." *Gaston County Historical Society Bulletin* 3, no. 2 (1957): 1–3.

———. "Hovis Woman Gave County Home Track." *Gaston County Historical Society Bulletin* 3, no. 3 (1957): 3.

———. "James Hillhouse White's Last Will and Testament." *Gaston County Historical Society Bulletin* 2, no. 2 (1956): 1–4.

———. "Jesse Holland Land Grant Described." *Gaston County Historical Society Bulletin* 6, no. 5 (1960): 1.

———. "Recalls Reconstruction Days and Iron Furnances." *Gaston County Historical Society Bulletin* 1, no. 4 (1955): 2.

———. "6,000 Federal Troops Camped at Clemmer Home Last Year of War." *Gaston County Historical Society Bulletin* 4, no. 1 (September 1958): 1–2.

Thomason, Randy T. Interviews with the author, including in person and e-mail over one month, June 2013.

Thornburg, Clarence O. Interview with the author. January 2, 1972

Thornburg, L.A. "Civil War from a Seventeen-Year-Old's Point of View." Unpublished manuscript written around the late 1800s and still in the possession of his family.

University of North Carolina. "Interview with Dr. William Clyde Friday." Oral Histories of the American South collection. Documenting the American South. http://docsouth.unc.edu/sohp (accessed June 2013).

U.S. Census Bureau Data, unpublished. Gaston County Public Library files, 1960.

Wehunt-Black, Rita. *Gaston County, North Carolina: A Brief History*. Charleston, SC: The History Press, 2008.

White, Edna Mae Pasour. Interview with the author. 1955.

Williams, Nancy. "Miss Nancy Williams Pens Family History as Eight Grade Project." *Gaston County Historical Society Bulletin* 6, no. 5 (1960): 1–3.

Williams, Robert L. *Gaston County: A Pictorial History*. Norfolk, VA: Donning Company, 1981.

Wilson, Morris. "Gaston Man's Worth Difficult to Assay." *Gaston County Historical Society Bulletin* 3, no. 3 (1957): 1–2.

INDEX

K

L

M

N

O

P

R

S

T

U

V

W

Y

ABOUT THE AUTHOR

Photo by Rick Haithcox.

Kitty Kay Thornburg Heller was born and raised in Dallas Township, North Carolina, where some of her ancestors have lived since before the Revolutionary War. She attended Lenoir Rhyne University and Salem State University, where she earned a master's degree in education. She also cofounded and was president of a research firm for twenty years. One of her joys in life has been working with young people and teaching them history. She received a National Teacher's Certification and taught in North Carolina public schools for twelve years. She holds a membership in the Gaston County Historical Society. Currently, she is happy to live in a place where old friends from grade school, as well as new friends, can be treasured.